The Best
Men's Stage Monologues
of 2005

The Best
Men's Stage Monologues
of 2005

edited by D. L. Lepidus

MONOLOGUE AUDITION SERIES

A SMITH AND KRAUS BOOK

Published by Smith and Kraus, Inc.
177 Lyme Road, Hanover, NH 03755
www.SmithandKraus.com

First Edition: January 2006
10 9 8 7 6 5 4 3 2 1

Cover illustration, "The Stage Hand," by Lisa Goldfinger
Cover design by Julia Hill Gignoux

The Monologue Audition Series
ISSN 1067-134X
ISBN 1-57525-429-8

**NOTE: These monologues are intended to be used for audition and class
study; permission is not required to use the material for those purposes. However, if there is a paid performance of any of the monologues included in
this book, please refer to the Rights and Permissions pages 108–114 to lo-
cate the source that can grant permission for public performance.**

Contents

Foreword

The monologues in this book have been culled from the best plays published or produced during the 2004–2005 theatrical season. Almost all are from published, readily available plays (see the Rights and Permissions pages at the back of the book for publisher contact information).

Many of the monologues herein are by playwrights of considerable reputation, such as Nilo Cruz, Stephen Adly Guirgis, Lynn Nottage, Lisa Loomer, and Michael Weller. Others are by future stars, such as Stephanie Fleischmann, Ruben Carbajal, Allison Moore, Jeanmarie Williams, Jonathan Rand, and Sheila Callaghan. Most are monologues by characters under forty, although there are a few, from plays such as *Ears on a Beatle*, which may be useful to older actors. I made a conscientious effort this year to find some great monologues that will be of particular interest to teen actors, such as the ones from *Chicken Bones for the Teenage Soup, Eloise & Ray, The Gifted Program,* and *The Moonlight Room.*

In short, this is the best darn monologue book I could put together. I know you will find in it the perfect piece for your audition or class use; but if you want some more options, check out Smith and Kraus' other fine monologue collections.

Many thanks to the agents, authors, and publishers who have allowed me to include these wonderful pieces in this book.

— *D. L. Lepidus*

ANIMAL
Kevin Augustine

Seriocomic
Jeff, twenties

Jeff is a shaman-in-training, talking to Eugene.

JEFF: *(To Eugene:)* You know, I haven't been hungry in so long. No appetite really. Too busy to make food. But these aren't so bad actually. Junk food. Just been eating a lot of junk food lately. *(He stops eating, grimacing.)* These have a funny aftertaste though, don't they? You want one?

(No response from Eugene.)

Not hungry right? You just want to sleep all the time now, am I right? How did I know? I know what you're thinking. *(Jeff stares out ahead.)* You're thinking, "What's the point of getting up out of bed again today, with all the work it's going to take to just get through another twenty-four hours?" Right? Another twenty-four hours where nothing goes right, nothing feels right, you just can't fit in, and it all starts to seem very, very pointless. So you start to think, maybe it would be better if I just . . . never woke up again. *(He looks over at Eugene.)* Well, I'm telling you, that's a good thing to think! Because it means we're close now! Because you're going to be the best! Because I saw you on TV! That's what I've been trying to tell you — I had a vision in my vision and you were on the commercial, in a blue suit — looking very sharp — and you said it's all going to change! Said "If it worked for me — it will work for you." See? So we'll be celebrating soon! Hey, are you listening to me? Sit up. Come, on, this is important. Eugene? Sit up. . . .

Eugene, what am I supposed to do? I've tried everything else. I've tried every depression support group there is, every double-blind experimental medication study they have. It works for a while, then they need to up the dosage, then it doesn't work, so they up it, then

1

I can't afford it. So I tried books on tape and magnets and crystals and meditation, but there are too many car alarms all the time — so I took a workshop to get in touch with my inner fetus and then a past life regression seminar — you know what I was in my past life? I was an Egyptian slave! That's what I saw, OK?! So none of that works. I can't go into the past anymore — I've already been there. I need the future. Something undiscovered and cutting edge! That's where you come in. So enough about me, OK?

ANNA IN THE TROPICS
Nilo Cruz

Dramatic
Juan Julian, twenties to forties

> *Juan Julian is a "lector" in a cigar factory. He reads to the workers
> while they roll cigars. It has been questioned whether or not the
> factory should employ a lector.*

JUAN JULIAN: Señor Chester, allow me to say something. My father used
to say that the tradition of having readers in the factories goes back
to the Taino Indians. He used to say that tobacco leaves whisper the
language of the sky. And that's because through the language of cigar
smoke the Indians used to communicate to the gods. Obviously I'm
not an Indian, but as a lector I am a distant relative of the Cacique,
the Chief Indian, who used to translate the sacred words of the deities.
The workers are the *oidores*. The ones who listen quietly, the same
way Taino Indians used to listen. And this is the tradition that you're
trying to destroy with your machine. Instead of promoting and pop-
ularizing machines, why don't you advertise our cigars? Or are you
working for the machine industry? . . .

Let's face it, Chester, workers, cigars aren't popular anymore.
Moving pictures now feature their stars smoking cigarettes: Valentino,
Douglas Fairbanks . . . They are all smoking little fags and not cig-
ars. You can go to Hollywood and offer our cigars to producers. . . .

I'm warning you. This fast mode of living with machines and
moving cars affects cigar consumption. And do you want to know
why, Señor Chester? Because people prefer a quick smoke, the kind
you get from a cigarette. The truth is that machines, cars, are keep-
ing us from taking walks and sitting on park benches, smoking a cigar
slowly and calmly. The way they should be smoked. So you see,
Chester, you want modernity, and modernity is actually destroying
our very own industry. The very act of smoking a cigar.

BAD BLOOD
Richard Stockwell

Dramatic
Tom, forty

> *Years ago, Tom had an affair with Catherine. She became pregnant
> and had an abortion — or so he thought, until the arrival of a
> teenaged runaway, to whom this monologue is addressed.*

TOM: Hallo, Jack. You stay right where you are until you get your breath
back. I've been expecting you for some time. Nice knife. It all worked
out nicely for you, didn't it? Belinda turning up. She looks just like
Catherine, doesn't she? She has her grace — I used to say Catherine
was a gift from God, do you remember? Which makes Belinda a gift
from — I don't know — from you, Jack, you. You finally gave me
something I wanted. I'm going to put the knife here, now. If you
feel strong enough, Jack, you go for it. I'm dying for an excuse to
kill you. *(He puts the knife half-way between the two of them.)* . . .

   She's so like Catherine. The stories she's told me about her. How
Catherine never forgave me. Catherine's pride, her fierce pride —
you'll remember that, Jack. Catherine would go through fire sooner
than lose face. The girl I abandoned, penniless, to carry my illegit-
imate child — too proud to beg from me. I ate it up, I lapped up
the tales of my lost love. It's a melodrama. A great crime of passion.
Except — like your dream of your great love affair with
Catherine — it really isn't true. I paid for the abortion. I did my duty
as I saw it then. Belinda told me all about that, all the hardship I
forced upon her and Catherine. Belinda forgave me, but Catherine
never will. And all the time Belinda was telling me these things, re-
lating my sins, I was inventing new ones — I was falling in love with
my daughter. . . .

   It's hard to describe to you, Jack, a man of such high moral prin-
ciples, but I was having — inappropriate thoughts about her. I was

4

lying awake at nights thinking most unparental thoughts — does that shock you? If you've heard enough, just reach for the knife — that'll put an end to it one way or another. I've longed for a child for so long, I've forgotten how to behave. It's hard to meet your daughter when she's already a woman, already a fully-fledged, fully-formed woman who looks just like the first great love of your youth. Look — you've always been slow — I'll push this a little closer . . . *(He nudges the knife a little closer.)*

What could I do for the girl I loved? I wasn't sure. The sin conceived is not a sin, it still requires the resolve to execute it. So, yesterday, I signed the will. It was an act of faith. I wanted to show that my love was real. Then, if my actions were to be misunderstood, at least the will was there to show my heart was true. I went for a drink — I needed a bit of Dutch courage — then I came back here and I seduced my daughter. Beautiful, isn't it? It was rather exciting. She's as soft and tender as her mother, Jack. I don't suppose she ever let you anywhere near her, she's far too scrupulous to let a worm like you touch her . . .

A BAD FRIEND
Jules Feiffer

Comic
Uncle Morty, forties to fifties

> *Uncle Morty is a TV writer in the early 1950s, visiting his sister
> and her husband in New York. They are determined leftists who
> think Morty's sold out by writing TV Westerns. Here, he is talking
> to his niece, Rose, about politics.*

UNCLE MORTY: Your mother started the Bronx revolution of nineteen
thirty-two which led to the overthrow of the czarina, and created
the People's Republic of Apartment Four A, 1235 Stratford Avenue,
with Naomi Klein Party Chairman. Now, czarina and party chairman are entirely different. Don't get them confused. In the case of
my mother, it was a naked display of raw power for its own sake. In
the case of *your* mother, it was a naked display of raw power, dedicated to advancing Socialism. I learned from your mother that anything you say or do is excusable if you claim it advances Socialism.
So when I left for my first writing job in the picture business, and
she accused me of selling out, I told her I was going out to Hollywood to advance Socialism by squirreling away messages in my scripts
so that the audiences who saw my movies could be enlightened. That
argument didn't go very far with your mother, but ten years later, it
turned out to be exactly what the House Un-American Committee
claims that people like me are doing — which, by the way, is pre-
cisely what *High Noon* is about. . . .

Oh, yes! *High Noon* is only a Western if you don't live and work
in Hollywood. If you do, it's a metaphor: this left-wing screenwriter
facing down black-hatted witch hunters. Isolated, friendless, in a town
owned by the studios — whose worthless necks he's saved over and
over — always coming through at the last minute with scripts that
pull them out of their money-grubbing holes! And what thanks does

Gary Cooper, this despised screenwriter who likes to think he's a cowboy, get? The entire town abandons him the one time *he* asks for help. The studios fall all over themselves getting in line to cave in as the Committee on Un-American Activities and its hired guns arrive in Washington on the noon train, armed to the teeth with subpoenas to make sure the poor schmuck never gets another writing credit.

BILLY AND DAGO
Charles Evered

Comic
Dago, thirties, a vagabond and streetwise fellow

Dago recalls running into an old friend.

DAGO: Hey, have you heard what happened to Tommy Rifkin? He's colonial now. I am not kidding you, Tommy Rifkin! Goofball "under the tracks" Rifkin from Vreeland Ave. is colonial — like you know, Ben Franklin. And as this is my hand in front of me I'm walkin' down State Street not seein' anybody I know, when all the sudden Tommy pops outa some alley way ahead of me and I see he's wearin' all that colonial crap, you know, like stockings and a triangle hat and those stupid pilgrim shoes and crap. I was sure it was him because I remembered his geeky walk — and so I remember he owes me like fifty bucks that he blew on the track a few years ago. So I run up to him and I go: "Hey, Tommy." And I swear to God he turns to me and goes: "May I prithee help you, sir?" Or something like that. And I go "Tommy, it's me!" And he starts lookin' at me like I'm nuts and so I just start askin' 'im where he's livin' and stuff and he says somethin' like; "I hold my estate in the great Commonwealth of Virginia, sir." And I go: "Yeah? Where?" And he goes; "Williamsburg." And that's when it dawns on me. Tommy Rifkin *is* colonial. He's turned into one of those weird colonial people from Colonial Williamsburg. I'm telling you, it's like a cult down there. Once you start bein' colonial, you can't stop. It's like a from of brainwashing is what it is, really. Tommy Rifkin. Colonial. What is *that* about?

BLUFF
Jeffrey Sweet

Dramatic
Neal, late twenties, early thirties

This is direct address to the audience.

NEAL: If you travel from one country to another, you know when you're
crossing the border. There's a sign, of course. "You are entering the
Sovereign State of Such and So." And sometimes some guards and
a barrier. This side of the barrier, you're in this place and the flag has
these colors and the currency has these historic faces on them. And
then you drive across a bridge and you're in that place. And you pull
out a passport and they ask you if you have anything to declare. And
they stamp your papers and wish you a nice visit, and on you go.
And now the flag has different colors and there are other faces looking serious on your money. This is how you know — these are the
things that confirm that where you are is not where you were. OK?
But the signs that you've crossed over into new territory with another
person, they aren't as well marked. Maybe you don't notice the change
itself when it actually happens. It's not like suddenly you feel aglow
or anything. I think maybe you just notice that something has
changed. It's something you catch up to a little after the fact. Maybe
you're starting to make plans, and in your mind the plans have the
word "we" in them, rather than "I"? Or maybe you find yourself reacting in a way differently than you would have before about — I
don't know — a song. A song that once you thought was kind of
stupid but now, because she likes it, you see all these levels of pro-
fundity and meaning in it. Like, what? — "Louie, Louie"?

BOISE
David Folwell

Seriocomic
Owen, twenties to thirties

> *Owen is a callous man, here talking to a man who works in the office where he works, about a sexual escapade he had with a woman at the office.*

OWEN: Dude. . . .

Val told me you guys were going to be here tonight. Merry Christmas. . . .

This company must have a ton of cash. *(Indicating drink.)* Free top-shelf, dude. . . .

I wore a suit. I wanted to hang with you, Dude. We never hang anymore. Oh, I wanted to tell you something. So, the other night, right, it's like 2:00 in the morning and I got nothing. And I'm horny as all hell. I walk into this total bridge and tunnel bar on Bleecker, for fuck-sake and I see Tia. . . .

Tia. Remember that chick that I hooked up with about six months ago? And she was, like, a stalker. I come over to her place and she was like fixing dinner for me and she had this cheese and she goes, "Oh, I got you this cheese you like because I saw you eating it the other night. And oh, I saw that you liked this beer so I got it for you. And we are going to have roast pork with apples because you pointed to it on the menu." . . .

So anyways, I get her to lie down on the bed. I was like, "I'm tired, you know. Let's lay down." And then all the sudden I'm like, I'm just not into this chick. I don't know why. And she starts to cozy up to me and I'm trying to remember if I took anything out of my pockets because I don't want to leave anything behind. I get an idea. I say, "Let's play truth or dare. I'll go first. When was the last time you slept with someone?" And she says, "I can't tell you that." And

I'm like, "Come on, I don't care." And then she says, "OK, but don't laugh . . . six months" . . . whatever. No fucking way. She's way too hot. So she goes, "What about you?" and I go, "Let me see, this morning." Which was true. I got Talia that morning and I was totally into her. Well, that did it. I was out of there in ten minutes. . . .

Oh, yeah, so I see her at this bar and she takes me to her place and I fuck her. So what's up with you?

BOISE
David Folwell

Comic
Bill, thirties

> *Bill is a middle-management type here talking to some other people at the office.*

BILL: Uh . . . well, uh, thanks, for the cake. You guys are great and . . . uh. You know, it's funny, I didn't want to come to work at all, today. I got into the shower this morning . . . heh . . the guy next door . . . they used all the hot water . . . I mean the shower wasn't cold, but I just you know . . . Like . . . he always does that . . . anyway . . . and then we . . . *(Looks to Tara and corrects himself.)* I was out of Apricot Bath Gel and I was like, why do I use Apricot Bath — so, I get on the subway and this black guy is like staring at me, the whole time and I mean. WHY is he staring at me . . . OK, I know why . . . I mean . . . everything, right? Whatever . . . I get off at Lex and 53rd and I . . . I start to . . . I get this feeling that I'm walking against a hard wind . . . There wasn't really a wind . . . or maybe it was like walking in Jello, or maybe . . . and this is probably it . . . I was walking against . . . my better judgment. That's it. It was like a hand was on my chest pushing me . . . But I kept going. I couldn't stop. I thought of going over to that skytram that goes over the East River. I've never done that before. Or walk over to that water fountain on 5th Ave and make a running start and use it like a slippy slide. Or, just go over to the bookstore and look at the photography books . . . or . . . skydiving books. I had dozens of choices I could make. I could get on a train, a plane, go skydiving. Anything. But I just kept marching . . . to work. I couldn't stop. And I got here and I sat down and just . . .

Yeah . . . I like burned my tongue real bad a couple of days ago and now . . . nothing tastes right . . . *(Awkward pause.)* Welp. Gotta get back to the old salt mines . . . Hehehe.

CHICKEN BONES FOR THE TEENAGE SOUP
Alan Haehnel

Comic
Kevin, late teens

Kevin, in cap and gown, as if delivering a graduation speech.

KEVIN: Members of the school board, Principal Clark, Superintendent Morrison, parents and relatives, and, of course, members of the class of 2004: As your class president for the past four years, I have had the privilege of leading and advising you on many occasions. I am grateful for this last opportunity before we depart to pursue our separate paths. And on this day of commencement, I would like you all to ponder one crucial word: Acceptance.

Who knows how many times and in how many places across this nation of ours this famous cliché will be spoken: Today is the first day of the rest of your life. I don't disagree with this quote at all. Obviously, it is true. However, I need you to understand the dangerous assumption hiding beneath this statement. The assumption is that, if today is the first day of the rest of your life, then the days that are to come hold the promise of something better than we have experienced so far. This, however, is not true. And that brings me back to the concept of acceptance.

My fellow graduates, I urge you to accept the fact that most of the goals you have for your life will not be met. Some of you are dreaming of becoming movie stars, professional athletes, great writers, wealthy lawyers, or high-ranking public officials. Given the social climate and families from which you come, though, these goals are completely unrealistic. Give it up.

Some will tell you that the key to success lies in fostering strong relationships with others. But you, my classmates, should accept the fact that your particular circle of friends and relations will do nothing to help you reach success. Holding on to these relationships will simply help you perpetuate your present, pitiful situation. But that is all right. You are who you are and, since birds of a feather flock together, you are not going to change anything substantially in terms of your relationships. In short, hold on to the friends you have because even lousy, inconsequential friends are better than no friends at all.

Finally, graduates, accept the fact that the habits you have now are the habits you will continue to have for the rest of your life. They, along with heredity and social conditioning, pretty much entirely control you. Accept the fact that your attempts to better yourself will be met with so much resistance, both internally and externally, that the effort is essentially wasted. Accept the fact that you are a slob and you are destined to become exactly like the slobs who raised you.

The sooner you can learn to accept these truths, my fellow graduates, the sooner you will be able to settle in to an unchallenging but not-too-bad life full of adequate food, bad television, and one or two major addictions. In conclusion, let me end with another amended cliché: Be all you can be. Just accept that all you can be just ain't all that much.

Thank you.

THE CLAWFOOT INTERVIEWS
Werner Trieschmann

Seriocomic
Jake, twenties

> *The overenthusiastic do-it-yourselfer Jake is trying to convince Olivia,*
> *whom he has never met before, that he's the right man to own her*
> *clawfoot bathtub and live with her for the rest of her natural life.*

JAKE: Sure, some *calls*. I'm here. In the flesh. I can pull it out myself. Let me lift up this end. No prob. I'm strong that way. I don't go to the doctor. I do not mess with those blood suckers. All I own is a box of Band-Aids and some rubbing alcohol. One time I sliced open my arm on this sheet metal. Got a nasty cut right down to the muscle. My supervisor begged me to go to the emergency room. Instead I went home, had some shots of tequila and sewed it up myself. I'm an independent, do-it-yourself guy. You're like me. Yeah, I've seen you out. I've seen you at Puritan Foods, getting those Soups for One. You bought a hammer there. Was it last week? Yeah. Not the place to buy tools, but I didn't say anything. I've seen you buy feminine stuff at the pharmacy. And those pills, too. I figure Valium or Zoloft. Am I right? No, I'm not *stalkin'* you. I got time on my hands. With the hammer, I figured you were hanging a picture of a boat. One of those catamarans in the Caribbean. I had fun thinking about how you were going to hang that picture and bang your thumb. I thought about how I should be doing it.

　　You know you got one of the worse houses in Pleasant Acres. Your eaves are a joke. I could hang pictures, install a water heater, replaster your walls, regrout your tub, restain your furniture, insulate your attic and weather strip your door frames. I'd make this house a vault and you won't need to turn on the heater. You could walk naked in the middle of winter. You got a nail that's come up right here *(Showing with his foot.)* and another one here. You've got

particle board under here. I can rip that up and put a layer of un-
derlayman and then a new floor. It'll hold up 'til our grandkids are
goin' ape crazy on it. Last for centuries. That's what's missing.
Permanence. And me.

CRASHING THE GATE
Frederick Stroppel

Seriocomic
Dooley, twenties to forties

> *Dooley is in a hideout with Sarah. The two are waiting for the go-ahead to blow up a building with a van full of explosives. Sarah has just received a call from their leader, telling her that the plans have changed. Dooley is now to drive the van into the building and blow it up, along with himself. In that case, he's asked Sarah, can he at least get laid first?*

DOOLEY: *(As he grudgingly backs off:)* It's just not right. I'm on an important mission here, I have to be at optimal mind-set. I should think if there were some small way you could attend to my needs, get me combat-ready, you would jump at the chance. Apparently not. Apparently I expect too much. . . .

Tell you this, those Arab fanatics, I'll bet they *make* their women service them. It's probably a religious thing with them. That's the trouble with America: Nobody goes to church anymore. No sense of discipline. That's why we're in the shitty state we're in today. . . .

We let these camel-fuckers waltz into our country, give them all the amenities, flying lessons and everything, and then they turn around and shove it right back up our ass. So how do we respond? OK, granted, we bomb a couple of caves in Afghanistan, but also, we start restricting our own liberties. Airport searches, gun controls, all kinds of totalitarian bullshit. Getting everything ass-backwards. We're the *good* guys. Don't restrict us — restrict *them!* And that's what I'm gonna say in my interview. Oh, I'm gonna lay some scary shit on them. I'm gonna do some serious mind-fucking. . . .

With Dan Rather or one of those *60 Minutes* guys. Tom Brokaw. Not Peter Jennings — he's a fucking Canadian. We blindfold them and take them to an undisclosed location — maybe here, that would be poetic justice — and I sit in the shadows, electronically disguise my voice . . . *(Using an "electronic" voice.)* "Remember Waco! Remember Ruby Ridge . . . !" It's gonna be so cool.

DEN OF THIEVES
Stephen Adly Guirgis

Comic
Paul, twenties to thirties

> *Paul — a man of passionate convictions who was formerly grossly overweight — is Maggie's sponsor in a twelve-step program for compulsive overeaters.*

PAUL: You're a Compulsive Overeater too, aren't you? . . . I know what you're going through. . . . You're overloaded with shame and guilt — . . . — Anger, yes! — . . . .

Don't open those Yodels, Maggie! Maggie, Goddamn it! Halt! . . . NOW, PUT THE FUCKING YODELS DOWN! I'm not letting you eat them for two reasons: Number one, they're stolen; and me and you are gonna gather all this stuff up and return it. All of it! Because that is how the program works. You called me tonight because you knew you had to reach out and that you had to return the stuff and make amends with the storekeeper. *Reach out and Return,* the first principle of the program. You called me tonight because you are brave, Maggie, you called me because you wanna turn it around. You're a winner, Maggie. You're gonna lick this, I can tell. Six months from now, you'll be leading workshops, visiting prisons, talking to youngsters at school. You'll be making a difference. Now, you could eat those Yodels and just give the guy the seventy-nine cents but I'm not going to let you do that to yourself 'cuz you're a compulsive overeater, aren't you? . . .

Look, you got a problem with junk food and you got a problem with larceny. You're already working on the larceny, and I'd be glad to take you to an O.A. meeting. . . .

Overeaters Anonymous, I'm an O.A. member. . . .

I used to weight four hundred pounds. . . .

Here's a photo of me on a horse. . . .

Now here's a picture of that same horse ten minutes later. . . .

I look at this picture every day to remind me of the pain and suffering, and in this case, death, that my compulsive overeating has cost myself and others . . . Back then, I was a mess. I smoked four packs of cigarettes a day, and when I wasn't sitting in front of the TV inhaling food, I was robbing this town blind. I was a big, fat, chain-smoking kleptomaniac. I was miserable. I hated myself. Hated myself so much I couldn't function. Have you ever felt that way? . . .

. . . Can I ask you something? . . .

. . . Do you like . . . life?

DEN OF THIEVES
Stephen Adly Guirgis

Seriocomic
Flaco, twenties to thirties

> *Flaco is a charismatic Puerto Rican wannabe of uncertain
> ancestry. He's telling some others about a big stash of money, there
> for the taking.*

FLACO: Check this out: my friend, Raheem, right? He got a friend, who
got a friend, who sell crack to this punk who works at this club, right?
It's a big fuckin' disco called Epiphany. So I go down there, right, to
meet this punk, maybe I can sell him some product. I meet him, he
starts buying from me — thinks he's getting a better deal with me,
which he's not — Anyway, I always meet him in this back room office on the ground floor which has an outside entrance. So I hang
there, do a deal, watch some Knicks wit' him; I notice they got a
safe. So I start coolin' with this kid on the regular, know what I'm
sayin', and he's at work, but all his job requires is for him to hang
in this office. I'm curious. So I befriend the motherfucker and within
a week — he's kickin' it all to me! . . . Turns out the club is selling
mad drugs; yo, hallucinogens, speed, X — they're raking it in. And
all the drug money goes in this basement safe. Someone comes to
pick it up every couple of days. They send the money to, like, Swe-
den, or some shit. The rest, they roll over to get more product. But
here's the thing. They're an independent operation! They ain't paying no one off: no Mafia, no cops no gangs, no no one! Nobody know
shit about it! I mean, it's gonna be all over for them in a couple of
weeks. But meantime, they got *money* down there. 750,000 dollars.
Someone's coming to pick it up at midnight, which means we got
three hours to get there first. Once we've stolen it, no one will care.
We're not stealing from cops or Mob — there's no reason for them

to know or care what we do. And the disco can't say *shit* to anyone because they'll be slaughtered if any of the heavy hitters ever know how much cash they baggin' without paying off. This is a gift from *God*, yo!

DEN OF THIEVES
Stephen Adly Guirgis

Seriocomic
Flaco, twenties to thirties

> *Flaco is a charismatic Puerto Rican wannabe of uncertain ances-
> try. He's telling some others about a big stash of money, there for the
> taking.*

FLACO: . . . Yeah well . . . I may not be perfect. I'm man enough to admit
it. I may not even be a "good" person. I might even be a "bad" person. I steal, I do crimes, I deal a little dope, I don't do any of those
things you just talked about. None of them. I smoke, drink, do alotta
drugs, fuckin' curse — if I see something I want, I take it. I mugged
a nun once. Two nuns! . . . I admit it. Up until now, I've been pretty
selfish and bad — and I don't apologize for it! 'Cuz if you grew up
how I did, you might be the same, maybe worse. You might be dead
right now. Maybe I didn't have the opportunities you had growing
up, but I ain't making excuses. I take full responsibility for who I
am. I did what I thought I had to do and here I am, still alive, still
standing . . . That's right. I am standing here with the one gift no
one's ever taken away from me and no one ever will because I won't
let them! I'm standin' here with a world full a *potential* still coursin'
through my veins! Look at me. I'm young, good-looking, highly intelligent, charismatic! I got charisma, baby! I'm a natural-born leader,
always have been. Can you deny it? I think not! I got so much potential, yo! I could be president. I could be a leader of my people.
Some day soon, I'll be a force for *righteousness* and when that happens, I'll move mountains! War is coming, yo, and when it does, the
good guys gonna need people like me, 'cause people like me, we're
rare! You're right about one thing, Paul. Up until now I haven't done
much to make a difference but my time is coming, son — my time

is coming! If I die now, the world may be losing the next Che Guevera, the next Malcolm X and shit, and they'll never even know I was here! I would hate for the world to suffer such a devastating loss, wouldn't you?! I'm a let your conscience be your guide, people. Finito!

DUTY HONOR COUNTRY
Stephen Bittrich

Dramatic
Bobeck, thirties

> *Bobeck is a thirtyish, white, National Guardsman from Houston,*
> *Texas, who has — very much against his will — been called up to*
> *serve in Operation Iraqi Freedom. In this three-person scene, Bobeck*
> *and LaBonne (an African American) have been separated from their*
> *unit, and are holed up in a trench waiting for daylight. To com-*
> *plicate matters, an Iraqi soldier who doesn't seem to speak English,*
> *has surrendered to them. Bobeck is clearly a contemptible racist jerk,*
> *while LaBonne, a more honorable man, actually believes in the mis-*
> *sion to free Iraq, but things are never as black-and-white as they*
> *seem . . . Bobeck's rantings actually make sense on a certain level.*
> *In this monologue Bobeck makes his case against the war.*

BOBECK: Look at this tattered motherfucker sittin' here. This is the big
Iraqi threat to the American way of life. Uniform in rags, hasn't eaten
a good meal in like a month 'cept rats, probably inherited his boots
off a dead soldier. Operation Iraqi Freedom is unfinished family business, that's all it is. And George Bush can kiss my lily-white redneck
ass. . . .

Oh, I can't wait to go hold hands with liberated little Iraqi children. Dancing in the street. Don't you get it, LaBonne? This is all
for nothin'. They don't want us here. They fuckin' hate us. Because
one, we support the religious zealots who aren't them, the Israelis,
and two, they realize this double-talk of freedom is all about Operation Iraqi Oil Freedom. And our being here will only inflame terrorism. It'll be like a goddamn hydra monster. Two heads growing
for every one we cut off. And even after we kick Saddam's ass —
which we will — some fuckin' Shi'ite motherfucker will step up to
take his place. Damn, man! Wake up! *(Beat.)* The one salvation I got

is that if I don't die tonight, in a hundred and fifty days my tour of duty will be over, and I'll be sippin' a Lone Star at Gilly's. . . .

Hey LaBonne, you know your man Bush — . . .

OK, OK, your man is Colin Powell. He gave a real perty speech at the UN, by the way. He's really lookin' after the brothers. But you know your Commander Bush in his first eight months in office was on the longest vacation in the last thirty-two years of the presidency. No shit. When Al Qaeda was putting the finishing touches on 9/11, GW was playing fetch with Spot, God rest his little soul. There were fuckin' memos circulating in the FBI and CIA about Arabs that were taking flying lessons with no interest in learning how to take off or land. Memos about terrorists planning to fly planes into buildings —

[LABONNE: Bush couldn't have stopped 9/11!]

BOBECK: Right. Because he was on *vacation!*

EARS ON A BEATLE
Mark St. Germain

Seriocomic
Howard, forties to fifties

> *Howard is an FBI agent, assigned to surveillance of John Lennon.*
> *Here he is talking about the time he posed as a telephone repair-*
> *man in order to bug Lennon's phone. He is talking to his partner,*
> *a younger agent.*

HOWARD: I saw his dirty laundry, for God's sake. He's a slob! And he never shut up! Maybe he was scared, maybe he was on something, I don't know. He says, "I'm so paranoid from them following me and tappin' my phones nobody will believe they're really tapped." By now, I'm really steaming. Who does he think I am? His shrink? His priest? He's my Subject! I said, "Hey! Stop the whining. It's your fault. Why don't you go back to England, stop wasting my money as a taxpayer on your damn trial!". . .

    I did! Why not? I told him, "The government doesn't want you here, so what do you do? Concerts for Attica, Anti-War Protests, TV shows bashing the same people who want you out; now that's smart, no, that's brilliant! Look at the food chain, pal. You're not high up there. Somebody's got to run the world, and it's not you!" . . .

    He starts laughing at me! Laughing! I said, "Hey, why do you want to live here anyway?" He looks straight at me and says, "This is where the music started. The land of the free." He was smiling, but I swear he was serious. He said, "I love this country. I want to live here." I said, fine. Good luck. Your phones aren't tapped, surprise surprise. Your whole block is having line problems, I've got a lot of stops to make. He said "Usually people try to break into my pad, not out." Then he asks me if I want a cup of tea. That totally threw me. . . .

    I said I don't like tea. Then he says "I've got beer in the icebox."

How could I turn that down? Not me, as me, me as Joe Phone Company? And meanwhile, I'm thinking, "Where's his staff? Where's his wife? Who's watching out for this guy?" But we're sitting at his kitchen table and he's cracking open a beer. . . .

He smoked. *(Pause.)* Winstons, OK? So there we are. I don't know what to say to him. "Ringo seems like a fun guy?" "Couldn't one of you guys come up with a real cover for the White Album?" Finally, I said, "My daughter liked your last record." He said, "Ah! So she's the one. Everybody else hated it. Did you?" . . .

I told him, "Just the songs I heard." He asks, "Which did you hate the least?" I said, "I don't know, I don't really remember any of them except for "Woman Is the Nigger of the World" which nearly got me lynched at my daughter's all-girl birthday party." He liked that. He asked how old she is, and I don't know if it was too many beers —

All of a sudden he's got me talking about Kate living with her mother. He asked how much I see her; I told him, "Not enough." Since the divorce? Sometimes I even hate to call now because I know her mother will say she's not home even when she's sitting right there because she doesn't want to talk to me. And he said, "I haven't seen my son since I left England." . . .

He said, "I hate calling, too, and every day I don't it just gets harder." I said, "You're John Lennon! You don't think your kid will pick up the phone for you?" and he said, "He doesn't care who I am except I'm the one not watching him grow up." And all of a sudden we're both on a roll, talking about his father who left him and his mother who got hit by a car and my father who doesn't even remember his own granddaughter's name and my grandparents who raised me and his aunt who raised him — you know there's a real "Strawberry Fields"? — and suddenly he grabs my arm, drags me to the phone and, says "Go on, call her now, we'll both say hi," and I did. I picked up his bugged phone and dialed Katie and it rang and it rang and I'm thinking pick up! I'm standing here with John Lennon! But nobody was home. And when I hung up he said, "You can't cheat kids. You know what they want, and it's you."

EARS ON A BEATLE
Mark St. Germain

Dramatic
Daniel, twenties

> *Daniel is a young FBI agent, assigned to surveillance of John Lennon.*
> *Here, he is talking to his partner, an older man, while they hang*
> *out outside Lennon's home.*

DANIEL: *Rosemary's Baby.* First thing I think of, every time I see it. It's a
great building, but I can't shake that it's where they shot *Rosemary's*
Baby. . . .

(Pause.) Hypothetical Scenario: A famous rock star invites an
undercover agent in for tea. The undercover agent has a beer. Two,
three, maybe; who knows? The rock star lights up. But not a cigarette. He wasn't smoking then, and he never smoked Winstons. Now
the undercover agent has a decision to make. Should he arrest him
on the spot? Should he get out of there and call in the FBI or the
NYPD to raid the place? They'd definitely find drugs; a few joints
at the least. Then what? The rock star would be charged and immi-
gration would throw him out of the country. So why didn't the agent
turn him in? Because he got an autograph? Because he had too much
beer? Maybe, because if he made that arrest his daughter would never
speak to him again? Why, Howard? Hypothetically. . . .

I learned a lot from you, Howard — . . .

You told me once — you told me a lot of things — but when
you told me about Bobby Kennedy and King, that first time? You
said it was our job to know. I wished you hadn't told me. I wished
I didn't know. But then I did. Now I know that's just part of our
job. The other part is sparing the world from knowing. Forget the
world. Sparing my children. I don't want them to know what I know.
I thought of you two years ago when the House formed their Committee on Assassinations. Four hundred witnesses, volumes of

testimony. I was positive they'd come up with absolutely nothing. But it was worse than that. Final Report: Our own leaders conclude there were "probably" two gunmen in Dallas. That President Kennedy was "probably" assassinated as a result of a conspiracy. That it's "likely" James Earl Ray killed Dr. King as part of a conspiracy. Kennedy and King: killed by some person or people we still don't know. Not to mention Bobby. So did the Country rise up in horror? Did we swear to find the whole monster and not just the finger that pulled the trigger? No, of course not. We went on pretending that by locking up one worthless little man we locked up evil. Because it's easier. And the alternative's unthinkable. You were right, Howard. Somebody has to rule the world. We won't. Can't. It's too much work.

ELEPHANT
Margie Stokley

Dramatic
Jay, twenties

> *Jay is in the passenger seat of a car driving cross-country to Arizona. He is in his twenties and a Lance Corporal in the U.S. Marine Corps. Jay has recently died in a car accident, leaving behind his parents, Henry and Kathleen, his sister, Michelle, and his seven-months pregnant girlfriend, Ellen. Separately, they all deal with their loss, and together, they are trying to find their way to move forward. Jay, as a hitchhiker, is revealing an anecdote with the hope that in sharing his memory his father will know he regrets not knowing they need him.*

JAY: No, that's not why it's hard to admit. I lost myself. I let them keep walking. I started walking slower. I wanted to see if they'd noticed. I can't believe I did this . . . I was looking in a window of a store . . . a liquor store. I saw their reflection cross the street . . . and I let them go . . . without me. My dad grabbed my mom's arm, and she immediately panicked and started screaming my name. I stood still. Frozen. I had begun something I didn't know how to get out of . . . I froze . . . and then hid in the liquor store. I fucking hid and watched them through the glass. I saw my dad pass the store and I started to cry. I was being erased. I was scared to walk out and have them see me . . . what would be my excuse? But my exit was prompted by a store clerk who knew I was too young to buy anything. As I crossed the street I screamed, "Mom!" I just kept yelling *Mom! Mom! Mom!* It was now their fault. They had disappeared . . . and let me go. How could they? I was pissed. Crazy, right?

My folks felt bad but my sister . . . my sister knew I was lying. I hated her that day for seeing through me . . . but today I hate myself for disappearing.

ELOISE & RAY
Stephanie Fleischmann

Dramatic
Ray, twenty-eight

> *Ray has recently finished a seven-year stretch in prison. He is pursuing Eloise, a teenaged girl.*

RAY: I am one of the BOYS of the boys of the boys of the one of the —
Blood-brother-dynamic-duo-action-packed-//in-cahoots-smooth-moving-partners-in-crime —

Boys.

One of the — The two of us. Him. And me.

Like sand and water.

Because it's sand that gits in my joints. Sandpaper rubbing them down from the inside out. Rheumatoid. Old at twenty-eight. Because of him. Jed. His legs to my lickety-split thinker slippin off and cementing my rheumy-eyed fate. Stiffin me, stashing me away in the slammer, seven years, leaving me there for my bones to calcify. Who ever heard of a cowboy with arthritis?

Some might say it was me who stashed myself. Me. Who took the rap and let him walk away because his were the legs between us. What was I thinkin? Momentary misstep, mammoth miscalculation. Seven years. Sandpaper pain scraping inside my head. Seven years. Adding up and taking over. So that all of a sudden it was time. To get even. To freeze him up. Wherever his legs had run their course. To throw a blow back in the direction of HIS stomach — When there she was. His. Even. Little sister twister shadow. So even. And me — I am — I was — One of the — She — is — She is a girl. Some strange kind of girl woman girl. All she gotta do is look in my direction and the scraping pain is gone.

So I got even. I did what I had to do, only I didn't expect — I mean — How was I to know what I would feel? Too much girl-woman-girl for — For me. So I ditched her. What else could I do? I came back here. Me and Jed. Small-town boys. Jewelry store hours from home. Nothing better to do than kick up some trouble. Here in Trouble, Texas, Scene of the Crime. Only — I been away from her one day and it's here. Sandpaper pain upside my head — Oh it's getting worse. It's bad.

What I need is water. My cure-all. Eloise. Me and her. Like sand and water.

ELOISE & RAY
Stephanie Fleischmann

Dramatic
Ray, twenty-eight

> *Ray has recently gotten out of prison, where he spent seven years, and he has returned to his hometown in Colorado, where he is becoming obsessed with Eloise, a sixteen-year-old girl. Here, he imagines a conversation with her.*

RAY: What I like about Eloise is her size. She's a little bitty thing of a girl. Compact, so you can fold her up. Put her in a box and keep her. Fold her, hold her in your arms. That she is small means she is more easily mine. That she is small means I can pick her up off the ground. Light as a feather as she is, as a cloud as a shroud. I can lift her high up in the air. If that's what she needs. Hold her, fold her there for a while. Upside down. Hold her upside down and shake her. If she needs to be taught. Like the time I give her the pearl.

(He imagines Eloise.)

RAY AS ELOISE: What does it mean if I take it?

RAY: That you're mine.

RAY AS ELOISE: And you? Are you mine?

RAY: I dunno Eloise, it's just a present.

RAY AS ELOISE: But what'm I gonna do with it?

RAY: I dunno, Eloise. For Chrissake. Eat it.

RAY AS ELOISE: All right. *(She does.)*

(He picks her up and holds her upside down and shakes her.)

RAY: She swallows the pearl. So I don't got no choice. 'Cept to hold her, fold her. Upside down. And shake her. It's what she needs. I give her that pearl, see, because a pearl is sand and water. I am the sand and Eloise is the water. We got both of the two right here. Both of the two.

(He stops shaking. Stares at her face hanging upside down.)

Ocean a million miles away.

(Starts shaking again.)

That she is small means I can lift her high up in the air. Shake her long and hard, until the pearl comes spitting out. A pellet of a pearl. A pez. My Eloise a pez dispenser out of order, pez pellets round and hard and sharp as BBs made of steel coming flying out of her mouth. Little and small as she is, my BB gun of a girl. So I shake her and shake her and the pearl comes flying out and she is crying and that's when I hold her close, never once letting her feet touch the ground. Hold her, fold her there for a while. Because that's what she needs. She needs to be taught.

THE EXONERATED
Jessica Blank and Erik Jensen

Dramatic
Delbert, fifties, black

> The Exonerated *is a documentary drama about real people who
> spent years on Death Row before being found innocent. Delbert is
> one of these people. This is direct-address to the audience.*

DELBERT: Mahatma Gandhi said that once he discovered who God was,
all fears left him regarding the rest of the world, you know, and it's
true, you know. If you're not harboring any kind of malice, any kind
of stuff like that in your heart, there really ain't too much to be
afraid of.

And I understand why people are afraid, I mean, I do think the
world itself, if you think about it, can be quite frightening — *(Pause.)*
I mean just like getting up every day, you know, I understand.

But you can't give in to that. 'Cause as they say in the cowboy
pictures, nobody's gonna live forever, you know what I'm sayin'? And
if you have to go, then you might as well go being about the high-
est thing that you can be about. And that means learning not to fear
other people, man, on a *human* level, white or black or *whatever.*

I mean, it's a real struggle not to lump all white people — you
know, if you're locked up in a room and a guy comes in wearin' a
gray suit and he hits you every time he walks into the room, afterwards you gonna have a thing about people with gray suits, I don't
give a fuck who they are.

But I try not to look at the world monolithically like that, and
that's what has helped me to survive. I mean, I think the American
criminal justice system is totally fucked up — I think some things
about our *country* are fucked up — but I also think it's a great country, you know, I really do.

But I mean, the fact that you can have people who probably

knew that a lotta folks were innocent — but *they* were not gonna be the ones to lose their jobs, jeopardize their kids' college education, blow their new SUV or whatever, for some abstraction like justice. *(Beat.)* That's fucked up.

And I know America gets tired of all of these people talking about what they don't have and what's wrong with the country. Folks say, "Well what's right with the country?" Well, what the fuck? To make things *better,* we ain't interested in what's *right* with it, we're interested in what's *wrong* with it. You don't say "What's *right* with my car?" What's *wrong* with it is what we better deal with.

EXPECTING ISABEL

Lisa Loomer

Comic

Nick, forty, Italian American

> Expecting Isabel *is a comedy about a New York couple trying to have a baby, by any means necessary. Nick is one-half of this couple. Miranda is his wife.*

NICK: *(To audience.)* OK, I'm gonna pick up the story and help her out. But first, you gotta understand something. I don't like to yell at my wife in the middle of Columbus Avenue — who does that? I was taught to turn the other cheek! Besides, you talked back, some nun'd pull your sideburns. And let me tell you something else. Until I met that hamster — I was a pretty happy guy! *(Glances offstage.)* Unlike some people . . . Sure I saw some bad things go down when I was a kid — who didn't? I saw Nino Gallata push his brother off a balcony when they were moving furniture. Palmer Di Fonzo — I cut off his eyebrow accidentally with a pen knife — his mother came after me with a gun. Hercules Sorgini, smallest kid on the block, broke his neck in a sled accident, it was like this — *(Leans head on right shoulder.)* For a year they called him, "Ten After Six." And Wee Wee Scomo had a heart attack right on the dance floor in junior high. Doing the Twist. He jumped up, did some splits, never got up again. Best dancer at Holy Savior. What are you gonna do? You gonna tell a kid, "Wee Wee — don't dance"? Besides — *(Glances offstage.)* If his mother had worried about violent television and the crap they put in the school lunches — would it have saved him from the Twist!? *(Yells offstage.)* THAT'S WHY I DON'T WORRY! *(To audience.)* And that's why I've always been a happy guy. Like when I go to the bank. I don't think, "Oh shit — *(A la Miranda.)* What if the guy on the other side of the cash machine's got a drug problem?" I don't even cup my hand over the keypad when I punch in my pin, which

38

happens to be "Jude" by the way, after the patron saint of lost causes — and not on my worst days — not even on the day my wife left me on Columbus Avenue would I have had a problem telling you that — 'cause, hey, if you wanted to go out later, and use my favorite saint's name to steal my money — *(Yells offstage.)* I JUST WASN'T GONNA WORRY ABOUT IT! Besides . . . *(Pauses, remembers.)* I didn't have any money. I spent my last fifty bucks on paint for the baby's room. And then we sold the apartment. Pretty fast too, because the couple who bought it were expecting a baby any day. Then me and Miranda had that fight in front of this Starbucks they put up where my favorite used art book store used to be . . . Then she went down to the sperm bank . . . *(Distraught.)* I did what any guy'd do — *(Pause.)* I went home to my mother.

FABULATION: or, The Re-Education of Undine

Lynn Nottage

Seriocomic
Flow, probably late twenties, black

> *Flow is rather addled as a result of his tour of duty in Kuwait ("Operation Desert Storm"). He has delusions that he is a philosopher and poet. His sister, Undine, has asked him about a poem he has been working on for years, an epic poem about Br'er Rabbit.*

FLOW: It is the exploration of the African American's journey. I'm exploding the role of the trickster in American mythology. I am using Br'er Rabbit, classic trickster, as means to express the dilemma faced by cultural stereotyping and the role it plays in the oppression on one hand and the liberation of the neoafric "to coin a phrase" individual, on the other. We at once reject and embrace —

It is this very conundrum that intrigues and confounds. We love, but we despise him. We admire, yet rebuke. We embrace, yet we push away. This glorious duality, enlivens and imprisons him. Because ain't he only hunting for "A way out of no way," as it's been said. And so you know, the poem is not about Br'er Rabbit — he is merely a means to convey a truth . . .

It is open-ended. A work in progress. A continuous journey. Oh Shit, what time is it? They just got in the new epi-lady and all the little motherfucking thieves'll be in tonight. I gotta roll in ten.

FABULATION: or, The Re-Education of Undine

Lynn Nottage

Dramatic
Addict #1, thirties to forties

> *We are in a group counseling session for addicts who have been ordered by the court to attend. The speaker is a former college professor who destroyed his life and career with cocaine. He is talking to the other addicts in the group.*

ADDICT #1: I miss it. I miss the taste and the smell of cocaine, that indescribable surge of confidence that fills the lungs. The numbness at the tip of my tongue, that sour metallic taste of really good blow. . . .

It was perfect, I mean in the middle of the day I'd excuse myself and slip out of an important faculty meeting, go to the stairwell and suck in fifteen, twenty, thirty dollars worth of crack.

(The addict pretends to inhale.)

I'd return a few minutes later full of energy, ideas, inspired, and then go teach a course on early American literature and not give a God damn. In fact the students admired my bold, gutsy devil-may-care attitude. Why? Because I'd lecture brilliantly and passionately on books . . . I hadn't read. Indeed, the university didn't know how high and mighty I was when they promoted me Chair of the English department and gave me an office with a view of Jersey. It was fantastic, I could smoke crack all day, every day in my office, seated in my leather chair, at my solid oak desk. It was near perfect, it was as close to nirvana as a junkie can achieve. But my colleagues were always on my case. "Beep, Mr. Logan wants you to attend a panel on the symbolism of the tomahawk in *The Deerslayer*." "Beep, Beep,

Ms. Cortini is here for her thesis defense, what should I tell her?" Those thesis-writing motherfuckers drove me crazy. And I wanted to kill them. But, you know what happens I don't have to tell any of you junkies. "Beep, President Sayer wants to see you in his office. Right this minute. Beep. He's getting impatient." Fuck you! But by that time I was on a four-day binge, my corduroy blazer stank like Chinatown. And I was paraded through the hallowed halls like some pathetic cocaine poster child. But, I don't remember when I became a criminal, but it happened at some point after that. The descent was classic, it's not even worthy of detail. Bla, bla, bla.

(A moment.)

One year. One year clean and I still walk around the city wondering how people cope, how do they survive without the aid of some substance? A boost? It makes me angry, no envious. How come some people get to lead lives filled with meaning and happiness? And I become a drug-addled junkie scheming for my next fix. . . .

Excuse me, I didn't interrupt you. Thank you. And you know what I think? I think that they will never understand the joy and comfort of that very first moment you draw the smoke into your lungs releasing years of stress, of not giving a damn whether you live or die. They won't know what it is to crave and love something so deeply that you're willing to lie, cheat, and steal to possess it. They won't know that kind of passion. I accept that I may go to hell, but I've experienced a kind of surrender, a letting go of self that years of meditation and expensive yuppie yoga classes won't yield. And I hold onto that feeling, fiendishly. That feeling empowers me, because I know the Shao-Lin strength that it takes to resist it, to fight it, to defeat it.

FLAGS
Jane Martin

Drama
Eddie, mid to late forties

> *Eddie's son has recently been killed while serving in Iraq. Here, he*
> *receives a condolence call from the president. Em is his wife.*

EDDIE: Eddie Desmopoulis.

> *(He listens.)*
>
> Whoa. Hold it. The real White House?
>
> *(Hand over receiver.)*
>
> So this is fuckin' over the top. . . .
>
> Yeah. Yeah. OK, that's me yeah. My pleasure. Call you Mr. Pres-
> ident, right? No way, I wouldn't feel comfortable. Carter, yeah. Hey
> no, I appreciate the condolences. Emma, right. Do for me?
>
> *(Hand over phone.)*
>
> He says what can he do for me.
>
> *(Back on.)*
>
> We talkin' seriously here or what? . . .
>
> Yeah, I got a couple things. He got killed doin' sanitation, the
> guy's a tank commander. No, I don't agree with that, huh-uh. United
> States officer pickin' up Iraqi Kotex, shovelin' sewage. I'm sayin' it's
> demeaning. Mr. President, all respect, I know what demeaning is.
> I'm a garbage man twenty years. Plus you put him in "stop and hold"
> after his tour like he's fuckin' drafted. No, you hold on a second. . . .
>
> They tell him put an enemy flag on this garbage place, which
> gimme a break here, we both know is bullshit, and the kid gets shot.
> My point?
>
> *(To Em.)*
>
> He says he's not clear on my point.
>
> *(Back on the phone.)*
>
> My point is you screwed up, my son's dead, they drag him

around deface his face off for what? I want an apology. No, "sorry" is not a fuckin' apology. Like "dear Mr. Desmopoulis, we screwed it up, we're at fault here, he should never been up there with the fuckin' Iraqi flag, he shoulda been home on normal rotation, deepest apologies." You know, clear the air man-to-man. You don't follow me? What the fuck is it you don't follow?

(Pause.)

Who are you? Yeah? Where'd Mr. President go? And you're what, a flunky right? Yeah? Yeah I got important business too. I'm unreasonable? Fuck you, hey? Hey?

(Phone goes dead.)

THE GIFTED PROGRAM
Ruben Carbajal

Dramatic
Steve, eighteen

> *Steve is a high school kid, and something of a stoner. Here he is talking to some equally maladapted friends about their school.*

STEVE: *(Suddenly remorseful.)* I know, I know, I know. I'm sorry. *(Beat.)* Shit. *(Loudly, but to himself.)* No wonder I can't make friends. *(To the others.)* I'm sorry, I just don't have that buffer, you know, that everyone else has. I say what I think, just whatever pops into my head. I think it's probably 'cause I'm stoned like, *ALL FUCKING DAY.* Damn, it's cold here. Do you know I've been to *eleven* schools in five years! I'm so fucking mixed up, honestly, I couldn't find this town on a fucking *map.* . . .

    This is the most fucked up school I've ever been to. This town? Fucked *up.* It's so fucking harsh and boring and cold here. I can't *take* this place sober. At least I'm anonymous. People forget about me. I know my mom does, teachers do. They don't even know I'm *here* half the time. Makes skipping class much easier. The reason I move around so much is my dad is like hunting down my mom. He's violent. He always seems to find us. I think my mom thinks this place will be too miserable even for him. I'm tired of trying to fit in. I miss California. That was the best place. We'd cut class, bring a boom-box and a bong to the beach, hang out, make a bonfire. Watch the sun go down. Make out, swim. I'll bet you guys never did anything like *close* to that in your entire fucking lives, right? *(Beat.)* I'm sorry. *(Beat.)* That's sad. *(Beat, frustrated with himself.)* Man. Big Mouth. *(Beat.)* It's so fucking cold, I can't seem to get warm, *like EVER.* I crank up the heat in the house, but it's still *there,* you know? *In the bones. (To Paul.)* But like, what am I trying to *say?* What you wrote here — this is some deep shit. You know? — poetic. I'm serious. . . .

No man, listen, *I'm serious.* I know about this shit. I had a friend in Cali that was into this really hot babe. She was like one of those hot West Coast blonde babes that like *hurt* to look at. It was actually *painful*, you know? *(Beat.)* So he like wrote her this letter on loose leaf paper, like a poem? He'd stolen most of the lines from different Led Zeppelin ballads, but I don't think she cared. When she read that shit? I mean she practically *creamed* herself. And I mean, like, bam, they were all over each other for like two fucking semesters. *(Pause.)* But the stuff you wrote? That's like *original* shit. You have to show that to her. You *have* to. I mean, this guy here, don't listen to him. This guy, he's bitter. . . .

(To Bill.) Sorry dude, *(To Paul.)* but I think *he's* threatened. I mean, I know I don't know you guys at all, but I think I can safely say that he has some serious vendetta. You gotta stand behind your bros, not stab them in the back, right?

HARVEST TIME
Frederick Stroppel

Dramatic
Mike, twenties

> *Mike is in the hospital, getting dialysis. His brother, Billy, comes to visit him, but Billy's more interested in watching a NASCAR race on TV.*

MIKE: Hey, what is wrong with you, Billy? I'm sick here, I'm getting my blood cleaned in front of your eyes, and all you care about is NASCAR? How about a little fucking sympathy, please? Is that too much to ask? What is there to *check,* anyway? The cars go around and around and around — it's *meaningless. . . .*

Where are they going? In a fucking circle? Think about that! I mean, get a *life! . . .*

(Beat.)

Between the two of you — NASCAR, hard lemonade . . . Jesus! *(Takes a deep breath.)* You're right. I shouldn't take this out on you. You're the only one who's coming through for me. . . .

And don't think I'm non-appreciative. Don't think I'm an ungrateful scumbag, because I'm not. I may not express myself, but you know how I feel. . . .

What happens is — you sit around all day, and you start to think. You have no choice. And you get philosophical. Because your whole life, it all boils down to one shitty little organ in your body you never gave a second thought. And now it's running the whole show. And everything gets turned upside-down. I mean, you're my younger brother, I shouldn't be needing your help. I should be giving you *my* kidney. And I would, I would give you my kidney, if it wasn't all fucked up. . . .

Or an eye, or an arm, or whatever. I'll tell you something, once this operation goes through and I'm back on my feet, I'm gonna do a lotta things different. I'm not gonna waste my life anymore. Because time is precious. That's something you learn. *(Takes Billy's arm.)* And I'm gonna take care of you, Billy, because you took care of me, and I don't forget. This whole thing, maybe it was a blessing. You and me, we could have gone on forever, all our lives, without having our bonds of brotherhood tested. We never would have known what we've got here, this special thing, this precious — thing . . . *(Starting to lose it.)* Thank God for you, Billy. I say it every day — Thank God, thank God . . .

    (Mike starts to cry.)

HAZZARD COUNTY
Allison Moore

Comic
Chad, seventeen

> *Chad is a white kid, a high school student. Although he's a middle-class, maybe upper middle-class Southern kid, he walks the walk and talks the talk of the ubiquitous hip-hop culture. "General Lee" was the cool car of the* Dukes of Hazzard. *Direct address to the audience.*

CHAD: People think it's cool, I guess. I mean, it's — you know, I'm out, and people know it's me, they know right away "Chad's pulling up," whatever, because, you know, not everybody has a *General Lee.* So it causes a stir, a little bit of a stir. I like that.

> *(Very exaggerated and slightly aggressive.)*
> "The Chicks Dig it."
> *(Laughs.)*
> Naw. I mean,
> *(As before.)*
> I mean THEY DO.
> *(Pause. Then smile.)*

I've been working on it for about 4 years. My dad used to race stock cars? He was an amateur and all, cause, you know he actually had a business to run, he's not some loser. But he's always working on something. And we were out one day because he wanted to look at this '68 Cutlass Supreme? So we go around back a this guy's house to check out his setup, and there it is, '69 Charger up on blocks. Total POS, engine completely out, but I flipped, because it's the exact right year. I was only like, thirteen, but my dad bought it for me for 800 bucks, which sounds like a lot, but. There's a lot of collectors. My dad helped me rebuild the engine, struts, all that. And the specs for the paint job are all online.

Some a my friends tried to make fun of me at first, cause I was like building a car I couldn't even drive? But now they're like "Dawg, that's that car is *rip*," and "Lemme drive it, catch some air, do it Duke-style" all that. My buddy Clay even got the Luke Duke Slide down, you know, where he slides across the hood and then jumps in the car?

We were out one time, on our way up to Clay's cabin, and we stop at this gas station. And this guy, total fucking hick, he sees the car and he starts in, just "Yeeeeee-haw!" All the way across the parking lot, just "Yee-haw!" like they did in the show. And Clay's all "Check this cracker," and the guy starts heading right for us, which I'm pretty used to now, and most folks are nice. But he's just this — got the gap teeth, and scraggly-ass hair, fucking reeks of, like, piss and Colt 45, and he's all "Lookie here! It's Bo and Luke! All the way from Hazzard County!" And we talk for a minute, and finally I'm like, I gotta go, nice to know ya. And I unlock the door and he flips. "You ain't even welded the doors shut! You can't have a General Lee with doors that open! Boy, you got to slide through the window." And Clay looks at the guy and says, real serious: "I know it never rained in Hazzard, sir, but it sure does come down sometimes in Conyers." And the guy looks confused, he's like, "What?" And Clay says, "Well, Bo and Luke could keep their windows down all the time, but my friend here sure doesn't want his interior to get wet when it rains." And the guy, just total classic, looks at Clay and says "Son, were you dropped on your head? When it rains, you just put the windows up, dumb ass!"

(*Chad laughs.*)

HAZZARD COUNTY
Allison Moore

Seriocomic
Blake, late twenties to late thirties

> *Blake is hoping to be a "reality TV" producer. He has been travel-*
> *ing around the country looking for stories about Real People. Here*
> *he is talking to a Southern woman he's met in a bar whose story he*
> *thinks might make for interesting television. Also, he's becoming at-*
> *tracted to her, romantically.*

BLAKE: When people find out I'm in reality TV, they always ask how we find this endless supply of "victims" willing to be filmed in such humiliating ways. And I say: It's like skydiving. No one believes his chute won't open. Otherwise they wouldn't do it. Every last person thinks "Sure, they made an ass out of all those other guys, *but they won't do it to me.*" They never realize they don't even have a choice. . . .

It doesn't matter what you say or don't say. We are not obligated to the truth. We are there to *construct entertainment.* We take any footage that is embarrassing, or sexual, and cut out everything else. And if you don't do anything stupid? We'll splice it together with something else. God, there was this barber in Indiana — this was for one of the thousand MTV projects I did. He was this ancient man with a huge mole on the side of his face, in this small town. And we interviewed him about his trade — very benign, what sort of clippers he used, and did he do shaves and what about beard trimming. He was the most patient man, which, in TV terms, is boring. So we started fucking with him, you know, playing dumb, repeating the same questions over and over, until he got frustrated and started shouting, "That's what I said! Men like a clean shave! It's got to be smooth!" And I edited the whole thing with footage of a bunch of strippers getting bikini waxes.

Shot of him shouting, "It's got to be smooth!"

Sound of a whip cracking.

Shot of the stripper moaning while being waxed.

Close up on his mole.

Shot of the stripper saying, "Men like it smooth."

Shot of him, "Well, yes I like it smooth, and so does my wife."

Shot of his wife raising her eyebrows.

Shot of the stripper spreading her legs.

That's how it's done. Did this patient man know *that's* what he was signing up for? Absolutely not. But by God, I got his consent.

KALIGHAT
Paul Knox

Dramatic
Philip, mid to late twenties

> *Philip went to Kalighat to work with the dying and destitute as a means of growing closer to Christ, which for him also means repressing his homosexuality. He left Kalighat because he succumbed to his desire for Peter. Here, in the last scene of the play, he has returned to Kalighat to say good-bye to Peter and to thank him for helping him to recognize and accept his true nature.*

PHILIP: I threw my suitcase in the river that night I ran off. Wanted to throw myself in too. I had nothing but the clothes on my back. I've been staying with a family of *hijras* in Park Circus. . . .

Eunuchs. Well, most of them anyway. They dress as women, and, well, they can be a little crude, but they've been very kind to me. They found me curled up under a tree in the park, took me back to their home, fed me, gave me a place to sleep. Made me feel like a real human being. They're such outcasts, but they take such good care of each other. And they took me in just like I was one of their family. Never believed I'd be accepted anywhere before, being who I am. Anyway, there's this man who comes to the *hijras'* house every couple of days. I'm not sure, but I think he comes for sex. Well, he's taking me to Kerala tonight for the Pilgrimage of Sabarimalai to the shrine of the boy god Ayyappa, born from the liaison of two male gods. Get it? The shrine is up in the mountains and the whole thing lasts a month. Women aren't allowed — it's all men. I'm told it's a very hot time. . . .

Oh, no. No no no. No sex for me. I'm saving myself for the right man. However, I am praying that he comes soon. I'm sorry I ran off on you like that. Wasn't very nice of me, I know. But I was afraid, and I . . . well, I needed to find my own way. But you helped me admit, see things the way they really are. How can I thank you for that? Here, this is my parents' address. I'll be headed back there after the pilgrimage. And I want you to have my tape player — my very last possession. Think of me when you listen to it. And, oh, here, this is some *prasad* from the Hare Krishna bakery. Karma-free baking for a conscious life.

THE LAST DAYS OF JUDAS ISCARIOT

Stephen Adly Guirgis

Comic
Saint Peter, could be any age

> *A petition has been brought before the court to reopen the case of Judas. Was he a villain, victim, hero, or a little of each? In this direct address to the audience, Saint Peter puts in his two cents worth.*

SAINT PETER: My name is Peter. They got a Basilica named after me in Rome, which is ironic, cuz, back in the day, if you even said the word "Rome" in my presence — more than likely I'd a beat you with my stick. I even had a standing rule on my fishing boat that was strictly enforced; "Talk about Rome, and your ass can swim home alone." I had to have those kinda rules laid down strong cuz my younger brother Drew and his friends — they liked to waste their time talkin' about overthrowing Rome and the coming of the Messiah instead of focusing on the task at hand — and I'd always be like, "Look fellas, unless your Messiah gonna come down right now and help us catch some *fish,* then, y'all need to shut the heck up and put your undivided focus on these damn *nets.*" Then, one day, Drew didn't turn up for work, then he come runnin' up to me at the shore at the end of the day when I'm bringin' the boat back in talkin' 'bout; "This is Jesus, bro — he's the Messiah. I ain't fishin' no more. I'm just gonna follow him" . . . And this Jesus, who resembled a Messiah about as much as I resemble a ballerina in a tutu, strides up on me and says; "Catch any fish today?" And I says; "No, I did not catch any fish today," and he says; "Take the boat back out to the Sea and you gonna catch some fish." So, I took Jesus out with me — intending to throw his ass overboard — but then he says, "Cast your nets wide and deep," so I did, and then . . . well . . . All I can say is I'm a damn professional commercial fisherman. No one knew the Sea and its tides better than me. There weren't no fish out there . . . but . . . that's because it turned out they was all in my net. And then Jesus said; "Follow me and I will make you a fisher of men." And what I didn't know then was that I would never see The Sea again.

THE LAST DAYS OF JUDAS ISCARIOT

Stephen Adly Guirgis

Comic

Saint Thomas, could be any age

A petition has been brought before the court to reopen the case of Judas Iscariot. Does he deserve to be in Hell; or, was he merely a victim of God's will? Here, Saint Thomas puts in his two cents worth. Direct address to the audience.

SAINT THOMAS: My name is Thomas. At the Last Supper, I was the first one to say that I would die for Jesus, and I was also the first one to head for the hills doing 90 when the Romans came and arrested him. And then, when Jesus resurrected himself, I was also the guy who said I wouldn't believe He was who He said He was unless I could see with my own eyes the holes in his hands and personally inspect them and touch them — as if I was some qualified medical examiner, like I was "Quincy" or something. But the thing of it was, Jesus showed them to me. And not only that, He let me touch them. In a ministry based entirely on the virtues of Faith, He gave me proof. I had no Faith, and He gave it to me for free. I don't know why I got the benefit of the doubt, and Judas didn't get help with his. And, I'm not saying this cuz I liked the guy — cuz personally, I thought Judas was a bit of a jerk-off. Actually, "fuckin dick" would be more accurate. Judas was the kinda guy — at least with me — where, one minute he's your friend, and the next minute, he's making fun of you in front of everybody. He used to like to say that the reason Jesus had to do the Miracle of the Loaves and the Fishes was because I ate all the food when no one was looking. Stuff like that. But then other times, he could be real nice, like, once we were partnered together to go into town to heal people and cast out demons, and well, I had some problems that day — everyone I tried to heal ended up getting worse, in fact, this one lady I almost blinded and another guy started going into convulsions — but Judas fixed it. He healed them — he really did — and that tells me his faith was genuine. And when we got back to camp that night, he didn't tell anybody how I messed up, in fact, he said I did a good job, and, I appreciated that. I knew Jesus knew it was bullshit, but I appreciated the gesture. I thought it showed largeness on Judas' part. And the thing is, Judas was kind of a dick, but he wasn't shallow or petty. He really was pretty large. He wasn't the best, but he was far from the worst. Jesus liked him, liked him a lot in fact. Judas was right up there in the top three with Mary Magdalene and Peter, who, by the way, could also be a dick sometimes too. The trick with Peter was: never talk about fish. The guy was crazy for fish. Say something wrong about a fish and forgettaboutit. The guy would go crazy. Anyways — Some people say Judas did what he did cuz he was greedy. Personally, I think that's bullshit. The guy wasn't wandering around the desert for three years with Jesus and a bunch of ragamuffins like us cuz he was looking to get rich. Other people say that The Devil got into him. Again, bullshit. Judas was loyal to a fault. Obsessively loyal even. Judas would have taken on The Devil and his entire army one against a thousand if he had to, and he woulda done it with relish. Other people say Judas did it cuz he knew the ship was sinking and he was trying to get himself a nut to have something to fall back on. Lissen: Judas was not a "fall back" guy, he was 100 hundred percent "fall forward." And to me, that deserves some consideration. I was not "fall forward." Not by a long shot. And neither were most of the others. Judas was a dick, but he deserved better. Just one saint's opinion.

THE LAST DAYS OF JUDAS ISCARIOT

Stephen Adly Guirgis

Comic
Pontius Pilate, could be any age

> *A lawyer named Cunningham has brought a suit before the court
> in the afterlife, in the matter of one Judas Iscariot, whom she be-
> lieves does not deserve damnation. Here, she has called Pontius Pi-
> late to the stand and is grilling him relentlessly about the Crucifixion.
> He's the real culprit, she believes, and history has whitewashed his
> culpability, history being "A lie agreed to."*

PILATE: A "lie"?! Whatchu know about what's a lie and what's the truth?!
Whatchu know about my history?! All's you got to go on is some
book written four different ways by four different Jews wasn't even
there in the first place! And whatchu know about my life AFTER
Palestine? Whatchu know about what I mighta did or didn't do when
I got back home to the Motherland? That's right — You don't know
jack — do you? They didn't write down that part of the story, did
they? Shit — I'm a tell you something: You and your presumptuous
nature reminds me more and more of my ex-wife Rhonda every
minute — and believe me that ain't no compliment! Yes, I met that
Jesus boy — seemed like a fine fellow! He dressed like a hobo and
smelled like a goat, but give the boy a shave and a shower, and he
woulda been basically alright. And I'll tell you something else: Unlike Judas, that Nazarene boy had character. He didn't come up on
me begging and groveling — crying like a bitch. He faced me like
a man, like a Roman almost, and that impressed me. I was willing
to just have him be clubbed in his head for a coupla hours — redi-
rect his youthful energies — but them Jews — they wasn't havin' none
a that! You can say what you want to, think what you want to, but
them Jews was fixin' to pitch a fit until that boy was served up for

lunch like chicken in the skillet! And they had the numbers on us that weekend — two hundred thousand strong converging on the city for they High Holidays and ready to rumble at the drop! I did what I had to do to preserve the damn peace! Why?! Cuz that was my damn job! I did my job! I did my damn job and now you wanna call me a liar? Question my veracity and my character?! I am a Roman, lady! One hundred percent, 24/7, we never close! Underneath my ball sac is stamped: VERITAS! And that means TRUTH! And that means my honor is defined by my integrity and my integrity is defined by my truth! And I defy you — here and now — to produce one shred of evidence to support your wild and defamatory claims! Shit! You better check the resume two times before you start tryin' ta sweep your dirt under a Roman's rug! I am clean like Dove and Ready for Love, Missy! I live in Heaven! Where you live at, girlfriend?! Shit! I'll tell you what though: When you get your head straightened out, gimme a call some time if you want to — I'll take you down to the Aqueduct for a Pizza and a Tussle. Show you my tattoos . . . Any more questions? . . .

OK then, I'm a roll out, now, boo — work on my short game.
(Pilate struts off magisterially —) . . .

PILATE: Hail Caesar, baby!

THE LAST DAYS OF JUDAS ISCARIOT
Stephen Adly Guirgis

Seriocomic
Satan, could be any age

> *Satan has been called to testify in court. A petition has been brought
> to reopen the case of Judas Iscariot. Cunningham, a woman, is the
> attorney who has petitioned the court. El-Fayoumy is the bumbling
> prosecuting attorney. Cunningham has pushed the Prince of Dark-
> ness a little too hard . . .*

SATAN: You know what, Cunningham: All those excuses you got wedged
between that dubious cleavage of yours: your mother, the bulimia,
the herpes, the booze, the abortions, the rape, the bipolar pharmaceutical adventures, the twin suicide attempts and the abject failures
at every relationship you ever attempted — all those things do nothing to Band-Aid the simple fact that There Comes a Time When the
World Stops Rewarding Potential — and when that time came for
you, you threw yourself the world's biggest pity party and dedicated
the rest of your short, pathetic, inconsequential life to finding fault
everywhere fuckin' else but in the return gaze of your own cosmet-
ically altered reflection. OK? . . .

El-Fayoumy, on a good day, your cock measures 3 and a half
inches erect and it goes off on a hair trigger if you so much as
sneeze . . . Worse than that, you're a Flatterer, and your Love of God
is utterly false — as is your hair color. And the sole reason you're so
hot for this nasty train wreck over here is because you're addicted to
tragedy and punishment — not because you *think* you're a piece of
shit, but because El-Fayoumy, the truth is: Your self-diagnosis is cor-
rect: You're a bag of hot air and a weakling — and you will never
ever be loved.

(To Cunningham.)

You'll never be loved either, Cunningham, and that's because you're incapable of giving it — but you already knew that about yourself, didn't you?

(To Judge.)

You can bring in the jury now, Frank. Never let it be said that The Prince of Tyre stood in the way of Truth.

THE LEARNING CURVE
Rogelio Martinez

Dramatic
Strand, mid to late forties

> *Strand is a history professor at Cornell. It is 1969, at the height of student protests against racism. Here, he is talking to one of his students, David, who is black. David is torn between his desire to get an education and his racial identity. Here, Professor Strand lets him know his position on the political demonstration that is going on at this very minute on campus.*

STRAND: That's democracy in action. Things are done differently nowadays. Forget old-fashioned values, hard work, merit — now anyone with a magic marker and a loud enough vocal instrument feels they have the right to tell you how the world should be run. . . .

Let's see the guilty party. Oh, of course. The usual suspects. Students for a Democratic Society — half of them don't even know what the word *democracy* means because supposedly they've spent all their college years fighting for it. COWARDS! You want advice, Mr. Jackson? Don't get caught up in the mess. Just last year some Negro students papered the entire campus with signs protesting the lack of Negro professors. They did this when prospective students were visiting the campus, so, of course, several of these students decided this university was not the place for them. Our community was hurt; our standards threatened. In their place, we had to accept students that perhaps belonged somewhere else. I will not let this university sink to the bottom of the list in some high school valedictorian's choice of higher education. . . .

There is a proper way to do things — renting a bullhorn and letting your hair grow long is not one of them. Now I have no problem with you . . . your color. I happen to think you don't belong here because you hurt the academic integrity of this university. It's very simple. Students can only be as intelligent as the professors that teach them and their classmates. If the level of discussion in the class happens to be brought down — certainly not by me, but perhaps by a question or two you decide to ask — then we all pay a price. Ultimately, you pay the biggest price because you will never get the answers you're looking for at a pace that's slow enough for it to make a difference in your life.

THE LIFE AND TIMES OF TULSA LOVECHILD

Greg Owens

Dramatic
Woody, early twenties

Woody is a wounded soldier. Here, he speaks to the audience.

WOODY: Some of us in the platoon used to speculate about the afterlife.
Whether or not there was such a thing and what it was like. Not
that we were really a metaphysically minded bunch of people. It's
just that the circumstances of our daily lives at the time sort of inspired consideration of the question.

One guy, Junior, from Missouri thought it would be like spend-
ing forever on the Lake of the Ozarks, catching fish every time he
threw his line into the water. Spud, from New York City, thought
of Death as an eternal taxi ride through mid-town.

I didn't know what to think, so I just imagined being stoned
forever. An endless loop of barely coherent, but seemingly profound,
thoughts and insights flashing across my mind to the background
beat of a warm, pleasant hum. Not a spiritually ambitious idea. But
it worked for me.

Only thing was, I turned out to be absolutely dead wrong. If
you'll pardon the pun.

You know what it's like? Believe me, I've had some time to think
about this and I think I've come up with the perfect analogy. It's like
being on one of those game shows where they put you in the sound-
proof booth. Forever.

At first I wondered what was going to happen to me next. Good
old Western linear thinking. Automatically assuming there was a
"next." A concept I've since abandoned. Now I just wonder.

I think about Vietnam. How many corpses piled up behind

mine? I wonder if anybody ever figured out a reason for it that they could live with.

I think about what I saw on television my last morning as a civilian. Those kids, terrified and bleeding in Grant Park. I wonder what kind of world they woke up to when those wounds healed. If they healed. The movement that Sylvia believed in so passionately. All those dreamers. I wonder if any of it survived.

I think about Sylvia. I wonder if she ever forgave me for what I did. Did she know that I too thought it was pointless and cowardly? And that I loved her.

I think about our child. What kind of world does my son or daughter live in? I wonder if he or she ever plays my eight-tracks. Or thinks of me? Feel how much I wish I'd known him? Or her.

That's what it's like.

LUMINESCENCE DATING
Carey Perloff

Dramatic
Nigel, late thirties, early forties

> *Nigel is an archaeologist and professor of archaeology, here address-*
> *ing his class.*

NIGEL: The reason it's difficult for our American friends to approach fourth-century military history with anything close to dispassionate analysis is that it is so oddly close to their own. Imagine the circumstances. The Peloponnesian War has been fought and lost. The rhetoric of democracy has crumbled on the battlefield. The Athenians have no ideological construct to hide behind anymore — it's every island for itself. So what does the Athenian empire resort to? Weapons build-up. Young men in uniform being sent abroad. Classic colonial behavior. Where Pericles had oratory, the second-century Cypriots had boys — what I mean to say is — they had a generation of boys who were totally betrayed — young boys — boys who knew nothing about Athens but were being sent to fight for her — while their families were starving and afraid — Do you see? *(He pauses, recovers.)* This extraordinary site on the north coast of Cyprus is riddled with tension. It represents generations of Greeks, building on top of each other, getting further and further from their democratic ideal as resources get scarcer and competition for those resources heats up. Look at it! The hypocrisy of the ruling democracy. The sacrifice of generations of sons, never to come home again. *(Becoming progressively more upset.)* How does it happen that children are taken from their parents? Why do we permit it? *(He looks around the room.)* And what happens to these children afterwards? Can you imagine? *(Desperate.)* Do you have any idea what it is to lose a child? Any of you? Do you? Can you imagine? Can you possibly imagine the pain? *(Pause.)* I think that's enough for today.

LUMINESCENCE DATING
Carey Perloff

Dramatic
Victor, mid to late thirties, black

> *Victor, an ex-dancer, now teaches history at a university. He
> specializes in queer theory interpretation of past events. Here, he is
> addressing his class.*

VICTOR: *(In a spotlight.)* The hardest choice in archaeology — as in un-
requited passion, I might add — is when to keep going — and when
to stop. What drives that choice? What makes you withdraw your
trowel and say — this far and no further? You crack the surface. You
hit the first layer. There are clues — suggestions — fragments —
you map them — treasure them — photograph them — and you
keep going. You dig further. You destroy the layer on top to get to
the one below. You decide — this is good — will the next strata be
better? Richer? More conclusive? It all depends on what you want
to find. If you're an Israeli archaeologist you dig right through the
Byzantine layer no matter how many gorgeous mosaics you find —
because the layer of the Second Temple is the one that matters. You
see?

And when you keep going — along the way — inevitably —
things get broken. Lost. Ignored. What is a valuable object on one
layer becomes garbage en route to the next.

(Pause.)

Example. Somewhere between Moscow and Petersburg, a man
has wandered in the snow, carrying another man's heart in his back
pocket. He takes it out at night to warm his hands, and it drops into
the snow. The heart sinks without a trace, a burning red hole in a
field of white. Now imagine. Maybe some day when the snow melts,
a child will find a small dried object caked with blood lying randomly

in a potato field. Maybe he will pick it up, and hold it to his heart, and wonder what it was, or what it might have been used for, all those years ago. *(Pause.)* Or maybe he'll think it's an old potato, and just drop it, randomly, back into the field.

LUMINESCENCE DATING
Carey Perloff

Dramatic
Victor, mid to late thirties, black

> *Victor, an ex-dancer, now teaches history at a university. He spe-*
> *cializes in queer theory interpretation of past events. Here, he is ad-*
> *dressing his class.*

VICTOR: We're talking today about *subjectivity.*

I was one of seven children. Vondie, Valerie, Varnel, Vinny, Vera
and Virginia. It was "one monogram fits all" at my house. The only
way for me to escape the mayhem was to join the ballet. My version
of the heroic quest for the self. And let me tell you, the trials of Hercules are nothing compared to standing on bleeding toes seven nights
a week lifting terrified white girls over your head to the sounds of
Tchaikovsky. But one night the epiphany came. As I was hauling girl
number five over my head in the second row of the corps, I realized
that the only thing I really wanted was to murder Sleeping Beauty
and kiss the prince myself. And that's when I turned to ancient
history.

I'm telling you this not because I expect you to care about my
personal life but because you should know that in my opinion, "ob-
jectivity" is a mirage. History is a story. A pattern. It can be read in
a hundred different ways, depending upon the questions being asked.
Sometimes the most amazing parts of it lie silent and hidden. If you
want to find them, you have to decide to change the lens and look
again.

Is this self-serving? Of course. We are all sifting through the rub-
ble to find a little piece of ourselves. Fragments that have been lost
suddenly re-emerge, burnished by time. *(Pause.)* Homotextuality. A
man sees a face in the mirror. Is it his own face, or that of his beloved?
The fact that men loved each other was more than a lifestyle choice

to the Greeks. It was a metaphor, a feedback loop, a journey into the self. The free flow of knowledge between like minds — for the Greeks, that was the ultimate method of making love. Discover the metaphor, and the truth cracks open. Like the kiss of Sleeping Beauty, the right touch of the lips brings the princess back to life. And that's when history gets exciting.

MAGGIE MAY
Tom O'Brien

Seriocomic
Charlie, middle-aged or older

> *Charlie is an ex-NFL owner. He has invited a young man named*
> *Donny on his boat. Here, he talks about his life. He also senses that*
> *Donny is in love with Maggie.*

CHARLIE: I mean, you're drinking Budweisers and smoking some cheap-
ass-back-of-the-school-bus weed. It gets old. But if you drink the
finest imported wines, have steak that melts in your mouth, scotch,
cigars, this beautiful Jamaican herb. It is happiness. This is it. They
don't want to tell you that. But here it is, my friend. Happiness. They
don't know. The people writing the self-help books? The "happiness
comes from within" bullshit. They don't got access to this stuff. How
would they know happiness when they don't even know what the
world has to offer? Do I look unhappy? Do I look like I'm search-
ing for meaning in life? Like I'm looking for a soul mate to spend
my golden years with? Fuck off! They're all golden years. I'm living
a golden life. I beat the fucking system, kid. . . .

And then my grandpappy made love to me in an outhouse. . . .

Just seeing if you're still listening. . . .

Thinking about your girl? . . .

I been there, kid. I know what you're going through. Don't make
decisions based on fear. That's death. . . .

Listen to me. Here's the deal, OK. There's all these lives out there
just floating around waiting for you to live them. You have all these
choices to make. Every choice you make splits things off into another parallel universe that's happening simultaneously to your own
pathetic reality. . . .

There's two lives in front of you right this second. A fork in the road, shall we say. Two roads diverged in the yellow wood. Which one you gonna take, Bubba, huh? . . .

Think about it. Most of the time we're too afraid to live. We say, "I couldn't do that. I couldn't be with her. I don't want to be happy." We talk ourselves out of living. But it's still out there. It's waiting for you. It's happening whether you choose it or not. It's just a question of whether you're gonna go for the ride or sit on the sidelines hopin' and dreamin'. All you have to do is step into it. *(Beat.)* A life unlived is not a life at all.

MICK JUST SHRUGS
Brian Dykstra

Dramatic
Mick, seventeen

> *Mick is ranting to his high school principal after having been*
> *caught trying to set up an art show project that would have involved*
> *burning an American flag.*

MICK: Pharmaceutical companies finance anti-drug campaigns in order
to keep marijuana from cutting into market share by competing with
their line of "mood enhancers." These anti-drug campaigns don't even
bother telling the truth. It's just total scare tactics, trading on stereo-
types that anybody who ever smoked a single bowl knows is total
bullshit. Why should we believe you about other drugs? You lied to
us about pot, half of you all are addicted to booze and pills, and way
too many of my friends were medicated with Ritalin or whatever
made raising them easier on their lazy parents. And, of course,
Africans with AIDS won't get a second look because they can't pay
for the pharmaceuticals. That's just tough, huh.

Sixty of the world's leading scientists (including twenty past
Nobel winners) have accused the White House of knowingly and will-
fully lying about scientific realities in order to further pro-business
and pro-military agendas. The administration's response up to present has been a big, fat "So?"

Companies get gift no-bid government contracts through political connections. Some states are considering not teaching evolu-
tion.

Laws are being bent and judicial appointments made in order
to further a Christian right-wing agenda that's more interested in Ar-
mageddon than people.

Environmental laws are castrated in the name of progress, so
rather than wasting profits on cleanup, corporations get to make more

scratch, while the possibility of a clean environment becomes more and more remote.

Global warming is joked about. But the ozone is depleting and we've lost almost 50 percent of the world's coral reef in my lifetime. I'm seventeen years old. If that isn't a canary choking to death in Dick Cheney's coal mine, then what is it?

I can't remember the last time we were below something called Orange Alert.

Political debate has devolved into partisan rhetoric in almost every forum. So truth is held hostage while ultra-conservative, pill-popping, right-wing assholes like Rush Limbaugh spew hate all over the airwaves and complain about something they keep calling the Liberal Media. Which I don't even know what that is. Do they mean Hollywood? Because they can't possibly mean MSNBC, or Rupert Murdoch Fox. They can't mean talk radio. They can't possibly mean the news.

The Florida National Guard was mobilized to illegally turn away thousands of African American voters in the last presidential election. Nobody had to answer for that.

In the name of fighting terrorism, civil rights are being denied citizens of this country every single day. And most of the time, we don't even know it.

We eat shit.

Intelligent people are marginalized by being branded "the Cultural Elite" while the government is reacting to polling that gets taken in Darwin's waiting room.

I haven't even really gotten started on Iraq.

MICK JUST SHRUGS
Brian Dykstra

Dramatic
Mick, seventeen

> *Mick is ranting to his high school principal after having been caught trying to set up an art show project that would have involved burning an American flag.*

MICK: We have people voting Republican who will never have even the hope of rising to the financial level where it might start to make sense to vote Republican. Habitually voting Republican, but who are, socially, actually pro choice and pro gun control, pro helping the poor, pro education, pro rights, but they vote Republican because they make more than a hundred grand a year and somehow the extra four thousand dollars they *might* have to pay to help fund a Democratic agenda is deemed too dangerous to the well-being of their bottom line.

    Democrats are wishy-washy reactionary cowards who allow their political enemies to define them. Liberal is a dirty word because conservatives say it is.

    Politicians from both parties are in the pockets of business because if you don't have a huge war chest there's no way you can win an election.

    The Supreme Court just proved it's either a totally partisan body, or for the first time, it's become clear just how fallible it is. Neither option is particularly reassuring.

    Our total dependence on oil has not only created the terrorists but it gives them the dollars and weapons they need to attack us. And, rather than address the reasons for their anger, we decide to fight fire with fire and burn everybody down.

    Jesus is suddenly the star-slash-victim of a sadomasochist snuff film rather than a loving and forgiving anything. Now ready to fuel more religious tension in a country in need of a handful of dogmatic Valium.

Can't watch the local news or read a paper because it's all about who died in what fire, what cop got shot, what rapist is on the loose, what politician got caught fucking the intern, and (in a related story) who screwed who out of what.

In this environment, the idea that all I want to do is burn a flag because I can't find anything else lying around that represents all the evils in the world, rather than gather up my most disenfranchised classmates, raid our daddies' gun cabinets, and try to break the Columbine record, should have you all heaping praise on me about my remarkable restraint. But, instead, just me mentioning Columbine is going to land me in deeper shit, because isn't it so much better if we just don't talk about these things?

THE MOONLIGHT ROOM
Tristine Skyler

Dramatic
Joshua, teens

> *Joshua is waiting with his friend Sal, a girl, in a hospital waiting
> room for word about an injured friend. Sal has expressed her fears
> about being kidnapped and winding up as a picture on the back of
> a milk carton. Here, he talks about a boy who disappeared. Not ex-
> actly reassuring . . .*

JOSHUA: So calm down. *(Pause. Josh stands for a second, looks down the hall-
way, and then sits back down.)* Remember Eben Macauley? He disappeared. Or was kidnapped. One or the other. No one ever saw him
again. One day in the summer between fourth and fifth grade I was
riding around. I saw him standing outside 158 on York Avenue. He
was doing the summer program and he was waiting for his mom to
come get him. He had just gotten a haircut and I remember his scalp
was really pink. And he was squinting his eyes, cause people with
blond hair and blue eyes can't see in bright sunlight. I waved at him
from my bike, and I said, "Yo Eben, what's up?" But he didn't hear
me. So I kept going and looped around the block and when I passed
the corner again he was gone. That was the last time I saw him. And
a week later he disappeared. His parents mobilized the entire city. I
think the mayor started a task force. There were posters on every bus.
His father quit his job. Their lives completely stopped. The only thing
they lived for was to find their son. They lived in the Pavillion. That
building on 77th with the pool on the roof? I'd hung out with
him a little bit in the summers, when we were younger. I would have
dinner at his house. It was weird, the way the whole family sat down
together, every night, at the table . . . They had this room, it had
white linoleum floors, and toys in there and books. It faced the East
River and at night the moon reflected off the water and the whole

family would go in there after dinner. They called it the moonlight room. . . .

(Pause.) You can't help but wonder. Wonder what it is to wonder. Not knowing where he is or if he'll ever come home. What that must be like to live with every day.

A NERVOUS SMILE
John Belluso

Dramatic
Brian, late thirties

> *Brian and his wife have a severely brain-damaged daughter. He has been having an affair with Nic, a friend of his wife's, whom they met in a support group for parents of brain-damaged children. Brian's wife is very wealthy, but the couple's marriage is dead, and Brian longs for escape from the pain of his bad marriage and the burden of caring for his daughter. He hopes to persuade Nic to run off with him.*

BRIAN: Have you ever dreamed of living in Buenos Aires? . . .

Do you want to know what our lives would be like if we lived together in Buenos Aires?

Can we just imagine for a moment? . . .

(Coming closer, his arms around her.)

A small home near Palermo Viejo.

The sun would wake us and the sheets would cling to our skin from the humidity.

I would kiss you, and touch your face, and brush the moist hair from your forehead.

A breakfast of dried fruits; cured meats, a little dulce de leche, I take it up with my finger and smooth it over your lips.

We walk together through the streets of the San Telmo district, shopping for things we don't really need in flea markets.

We stroll through the Recoleta Cemetery.

A sprawling maze of mausoleums; intricate, dramatic, haunting.

Black steel gates, towering statues of Angels and the Virgin Mary looking down over the catacombs, looking down over us.

And the food!

Oh god, we will get fat together. The beef, the *beef . . . !*

The beef is incomprehensibly good, tender and smooth, strands of it falling off the bone and melting on your tongue . . .

Mixed olives and red peppers, warm round sweet breads, red wine and smoked cheeses and nuts . . .

And we'll tango in the streets outside the Plaza Dorrego!

We'll dance till we are exhausted, and then we'll take off our shoes and walk through the grass, the landscaped parks, under white moonlight.

And back in our home step out onto our balcony and we'll watch the lights of the city from above, the beautiful people moving through the streets, and no one will hurt us or judge us or hate us for our sins.

We will be Undivided.

THE PEOPLE VS. SPAM
Jonathan Rand

Seriocomic
The Defense, could be any age

> *Here, The Defense presents its case in a most controversial trial —*
> *America is suing the junk e-mail industry.*

THE DEFENSE: Your Honor, members of the jury; members of . . . America. I come before you today to protest a grave injustice. Imagine, if
you will, the following scenario: You're walking up and down the aisles
of your local supermarket. Suddenly, an intense craving hits you. You
decide: What I want right this moment, more than anything in the
world, is a thick, juicy steak. So naturally, you do what any decent
American would do. You push your shopping cart to the meat section, peruse your options with the friendly man at the counter —
whose name is Jim — and decide upon the perfect cut of meat. Sound
normal so far? It sure does to me. But no, just as Jim bestows you
with the juiciest slab of steak money can buy, just as you are mere
seconds from placing it in your cart, a hand appears out of nowhere.
This hand wrenches the steak from your grasp — the steak you so
desire; the steak you deserve after toiling fifty, sixty, one hundred
hours every week for your country; that steak, dripping with the
blood of the brave soldiers who fought for our independence some
200 years ago — that very hand removes the steak from your possession, throws it to the floor, kicks it, then looks up and spits in
your eye.

Ladies and gentlemen of the jury . . . This story I present to
you is no metaphor. It is an allegory. The steak of which I speak represents the products you desire every day. The man at the meat
counter, Jim, represents all honest, hard-working Americans who wish
to give you the products you so deserve, be it at a supermarket, or
in the inbox of your personal computer. Lastly, the hand which

impinged upon your very freedom in the meat section? That hand sits in this courtroom today. That hand is trying to take away the American people's right to receive legitimate e-mail correspondence from respectable vendors across this great land — vendors who wish nothing more than to give you the products you deserve. Products which make us better people, better citizens, and better members . . . of the human race.

Ladies and gentlemen of the jury, you may be thinking to yourself: How could such an atrocity happen in this land of the free? Surely a civilized nation such as America couldn't possibly stoop so low as to rip away our most basic human rights. You might expect such acts of injustice in developing countries like Zimbabwe or Canada. But the United States of America? Within these majestic purple mountains? Above these plains of fruit? I would hope not. I would certainly hope not. America . . . America . . . these plaintiffs shed their DISgrace on thee.

Thank you.

PLATONOV! PLATONOV! PLATONOV!

Eric Michael Kochmer

Comic
Osip, twenties to thirties

This play is a hilarious send-up of Chekhov. Here Osip, a horse thief,
is talking to Sasha, Platonov's wife, who has asked him about a failed
romance.

OSIP: How was this misery birthed in me? It happened with the simplicity of a fable. The vision . . . it comes to me . . . I'm walking down a trail in the woodland, not far from here . . . through the branches I spot the WIDOW standing upright in the cold spring water, her dress tucked up as to not get her dry clothes wet . . . and . . . and . . . and she's scooping up water with a leaf! Ha! Ha! Ha! Scoop it up . . . scoop it up . . . scoop it up and drink it down your throat! Ha! Ha! Ha! And then she drowns her whole head in it . . . die for me my love die for me . . . so I walk down to the waterside right up close to her and she doesn't look at me at all . . . as if saying "SCOUNDREL! WHY SHOULD I EVEN LOOK AT YOU AT ALL!" "LADY," says I, "I just see you're having a fresh cold drink of clean water. . . ." "What business is it of yours?" she says. "Get on out of here you dirty unworthy shameful unabashed swarthy peasant." Never even looked at me twice. Well, I must say I was frightened and hurt, and ashamed of being a peasant. "What are you staring at me for, fool? Never seen a woman before have you . . . or perhaps you've taken a liking to me?" "Oh yes!" says I. "Well . . . well . . . I like you! I like you a whole lot!" Says I. "You're a noble, sensitive, warmhearted individual, you're beautiful. Never in my life have I seen a more beautiful lady: Manka, our local beauty, the constable's daughter," says I, "Next to you? — why she's merely a donkey, a water snake, a chicken . . . a dead rotten chicken! You're so delicate! Why if I kissed you right now . . ." "Go ahead," she says. "Kiss me if you want to . . ." Since then, interestingly enough, I seem to have lost my mind. AND I HAVE BEEN BANISHED INTO THIS CRUEL WORLD OF MADNESS! . . . I'm going to shred the skin from this very flesh, my beloved Sasha . . . It's been such a long time since I've said grace . . . Her eyes are always there before me . . . when I sleep . . . when I eat these wonderful potatoes . . . when . . . when . . . when . . . AHHHHHHHHH!!! "Go ahead, scoundrel," she whispers. "Kiss me, you rank beast kiss me right on the lips with your power," and she giggles at me . . . Ahhhhhhhh! I feel like goring myself in the heart with a knife or ripping off my very head . . . I began doing anything she demanded. I killed a penguin for her. I captured a rooster, I refurnished her entire estate with stolen goods that took me many many many many many months to steal. I even brought her a live bear once. I tried to satisfy her every instance . . . everything she told me to do I did . . . I did . . . I DID! . . . Even if she told me to baste myself over a spit . . . I would have done it, Sasha . . . I WOULD HAVE DONE IT!!! . . . So Sasha, beautiful noble Sasha who is married to that bastard clown . . . I kept on going to her house, like a sick pedophile. Sometime ago I brought her a chicken, a rubber chicken, "Look at what I have brought to you, my worship . . . my only love . . . my only life," says I. "Look at this rubber chicken I brought you! Isn't it wonderful! Isn't it beautiful! WHY, ISN'T IT JUST A DREAM?" She just looked at me and stared with those sad wonderful eyes. "They say you're a villainous burglar, Osip, do they lie?" "They wouldn't lie to you my lovely . . ." says I. "We have to fix you," she said . . . "We have to fix you." Reform . . . but I'm a sick madman. "Off you go on a journey to Moscow. Go. And in a year you'll come home a different person." Once a rubber chicken, always a rubber chicken.

PORTRAITS
Jonathan Bell

Dramatic
Daniel, thirties to forties

> *Daniel has been having an affair with a woman named Amanda,*
> *with whom he was shacking up when the planes hit the World Trade*
> *Center, where he should have been the morning of September 11,*
> *2001.*

DANIEL: The truth was that Kate and I didn't care. She laughed about my
mother. She just couldn't believe someone like that actually existed.
And I ignored the "rich boy" comments from cops and fireman at
the barbecues at Breezy Point. We had two boys in three years. I was
making money . . . Life was grand and precious . . . and I was too
stupid to appreciate it. I'm not going to bore you with details about
pissing my great life away over twenty years. I might have become
a repentant man in my fifties, walking the beach with my regrets.
Kate and I had fights, and there were drinks thrown in my face, but
she . . . appeared to be along for the whole ride. She may not have
been in love with me anymore, but I don't think she would have put
my sons or her family through a divorce, and she's Catholic, so . . .
Only one problem, one huge mistake . . . Amanda.

She was a female version of me. She liked danger, married men,
and . . . sex. It was kind of a sickness really. We didn't love each other.
I was sexually dependent on her. We'd get a hotel room, have great
sex, then I couldn't wait to get rid of her. She didn't care. We didn't
socialize. We'd just meet and fuck. If it weren't me, it would be some
other . . . There was uh . . . a turn of events that ended our . . . relationship. I was usually in the office at seven-thirty every morning.
This particular Tuesday morning, Kate was out of town visiting one
of our boys at college. This gave me the opportunity to hook up with
Amanda on a Monday night. We got a suite at The Pierre, and even

spent the night together. We celebrated with a couple of bottles of Crystal, and had a long night of sex, so I was pretty foggy that morning. I woke up a little after nine to the sound of my cell phone ringing. It was Kate. She asked me where I was, and if I was all right. I said, "Of course I'm all right. I'm sitting at my desk" . . . There was a long pause. Then she said, "You son of a bitch. Your office is a fireball. People are dying. I hope she was worth it." . . . She hung up. And I . . . I was caught in an unthinkable lie.

PURE CONFIDENCE
Carlyle Brown

Seriocomic
Simon, twenties, black

> *Simon is a slave. He is also a gifted jockey, and he hopes to parlay
> his genius at riding into freedom and a piece of the American pie.
> He is telling Caroline, also a slave, whom he hopes to wed, about
> a race he has won.*

SIMON: Caroline! Come on in girl. I'm riding this barrel in the freedom
stakes. Freedom against Slavery, match race, winner takes all. Simon
Cato on Freedom and the Bondage Man riding Slavery. And with a
tap of the drum they're off. Oops Freedom got a bad start, Slavery's
in the lead. Coming around the first turn it's Slavery by a length.
Freedom holding steady, storm clouds are a coming, and the patter
of rain falling on the track. Down the backstretch the thunder begins to roll as the rain starts poring down. It don't look good for Freedom, 'cause Slavery is a mudder. The dirtier and more murky it gets
the better she likes it and she's running like a hellhound on judgment day. Coming around the far turn it's Slavery by half a length,
Freedom is gaining. Passing the grandstand it's Freedom and Slavery neck and neck, Slavery on the inside, Freedom on the outside,
side by side, not sign a daylight between 'em. "Give it up," says the
Bondage Man, "You can't win today." "Ain't no way," says
Simon Cato, "you soon to be looking at my horse's ass." And Slavery is running, and Freedom is running, and the mud is flying and
you can't tell which rider is white and which rider is black or which
horse is which. First it's Slavery by a nose, then Freedom by nose,
now it's Slavery by a neck and then Freedom by a neck, back and
forth round the near turn and down the back stretch. The Bondage
Man got his spurs dug into Slavery's sides, and he's whipping her
flanks like the devil beating off justice. And Simon Cato is riding

low and biding his time. And coming round again on the far turn he lays down his whip and calls on Freedom to give him all her best and she starts to running like pure moonshine swallowing down your throat. Coming off the turn it's Freedom by half a length, Freedom by a whole length, Freedom by two lengths, three lengths, four lengths. It's Freedom and Simon Cato the winners . . . Slavery to place and ain't nobody to show. And the crowd roars. *(Simon makes a sound of a crowd roaring.)* Mister Reporter man from the Louisville Gazette asks Simon, "Boy how you win that race?" Go on Caroline, you be the reporter. Ask me how I won that race on Freedom. . . .

Well, you see I take my little self on top of my big horse and we run faster then them other little fellows on top of their big horses, and then I win. Say, "Fascinating mister Cato, fascinating, fascinating." . . .

No, you need one more fascinating in there . . . There's three . . . "Fascinating mister Cato, fascinating, fascinating." . . .

Thank-you, thank-you, thank-you . . .

SMALL TRAGEDY
Craig Lucas

Dramatic
Hakia, twenties

> *Hakia, a refugee from Yugoslavia, has been cast in the title role in*
> *a college theater production of* Oedipus Rex. *He is talking to Jen,*
> *a fellow actor, who has asked him about the war in Yugoslavia.*

HAKIA: Your friend asked me if there wasn't "like a sort of a war going
on" in my country. . . .

Not to put too fine a point on it — or risk bringing anyone
down — but two hundred thousand of my countrymen, including
all of my family, were slaughtered in full view of the world. Our
Christian neighbors, who have known us since childhood, for generations — and mind you, these are not peasants, poor people, these
are doctors and successful businessmen and lawyers and scientists,
my father was a Professor of Philosophy, *indistinguishable* from you
or me if you were to see them which you couldn't or refused to, I won't
speak for you. Americans refused — these people, friends, colleagues,
simply because they had Serbian ancestry and we were Muslims, came
into our homes, murdered many of the men, raped the women and
drove the survivors into camps where most starved to death. That is
not, nowhere near the worst. If I were to tell you the worst of what
I saw, you would say I was inventing it. Not possible. . . .

The only people in the world capable of putting a stop to any
of this left an embargo on all weapons to one side, ours, and stood
by, using so-called Humanitarian Efforts to excuse themselves from
doing anything. . . .

You're, as I said, interested in winning. If we agree, *together,* not
to see something, then . . . Well . . . And just to be perfectly clear:
an American is what I want very much to become; it is only because
of American relief efforts, private — . . .

I am alive at all.

SMALL TRAGEDY
Craig Lucas

Dramatic
Nathaniel, could be any age

> *Nathaniel is the director of a college theater production of* Oedipus
> Rex. *Here, he talks to the cast about his particular take on the play.*

NATHANIEL: If you were going, I were going to take a particular, you know,
slant on the play — I mean, that would be the one I'd — and I'm
not going to do that. I hate that in productions where you can see
the goddamn point of view of the director like handprints from a
blind person feeling their way around the set after they've fallen into
paint: You see?, it's all about the "Riddle of Human Identity" — who
are we? It's all about repression, right????, and the Freudians all leap
up and cheer, or it's about rootlessness, homelessness! Oedipus, poor
thing, is thrust out of his warm home as an infant no less and then
he's thrust out again, for good, and blind no less, as an adult! Social
workers, take note. And socialists. Or it's about the civilized versus
the bestial, our cultural, learned behavior in opposition to the sav-
age creature within who must then be cast out, the scapegoat, you
see! Tragedy itself, the word, is based on this: the goat! Goat festival, or some fucking thing, Paola can tell you. OR OR it's about pol-
lution, inside and out, OR as some, one of us suggested Oedipus is
Athens, read "America," get it?!?, or it's about the search for the ultimate meaning, is suffering what gives us meaning or is it the search
for meaning that causes us to suffer so much?!? OR, is it all some
juridical debate as to which laws are still appropriate — all the ACLU-
ers would line up around the block. That shit is easy! Oh, wow, he's
saying it is a random universe or do the gods have a plan, no matter how inscrutable! You'd win an Obie for that. And and . . . I don't
know . . . I'm . . .

I've finished grinding my ax.

THE TAXI CABARET
Peter Mills

Comic
Zach, twenty-something

> The Taxi Cabaret *is a musical about twenty-something singles in the Big City. Zach, while driving, expresses road rage.*

ZACH: Jeez . . . *(He flips off the radio. After a moment, He begins looking around.)* Baby On Board . . . am I supposed to care? If I'm careening out of control down the highway and it comes down to either hitting your car or going over the embankment, am I supposed to see that sticker and say to myself, "No — not the baby!" I got news for you, lady. If I were in a monster truck right now, I would drive over your little SUV, baby and all, just to get the hell out of this mess. Uh, hi, buddy — are you merging? I don't think you are. Mean People Suck — that's a good one. I bet your boss is a real mean guy, and you just can't figure out why he's the boss and you're the pathetic underling with the Hyundai. Well, I know why. It's because mean people get things done. Do you think Alexander the Great said, "I have a chance to conquer the world here, but, gee, that'd be awfully mean to certain people . . ." Mean people are out there moving mountains, and you can't even merge. You know what does suck? Traffic. There's too many people on this island. And everyone's got their little manifesto that the whole world's gotta know about: I'm Pro-Life . . . I'm anti-fur . . . I'm queer and I'm here . . . I'm against guns . . . I love cats . . . Just shut up! There are no bumper stickers on my car. I know who I am, and that's enough. I have nothing to say to you people.

THE TAXI CABARET
Peter Mills

Comic
Scott, twenty-something

> The Taxi Cabaret *is a musical about twenty-something singles in
> the Big City. In this direct address to the audience, Scott, an aspir-
> ing novelist, talks about his writer's block.*

SCOTT: I was out walking all morning, still trying to find that great opening line for my novel. As of today, I've been in this city a year. One
full year . . . zero inspiration. And I couldn't figure out why. I mean,
they say you have to suffer to write, and here I've been suffering up
a storm, but — nothing's come of it. So today I was gonna just walk
until I saw something to inspire me. Well, I walked all the way up
from the Village up to East 72nd Street, and I must have tried out
maybe a hundred different beginnings. Everything I saw was a
story . . . a tragic romance for the pretzel man, a tale of corporate
intrigue in the Met Life building, a delightful children's book about
a dogwalker who can understand dog language. There were so many
beginnings, but none of them went anywhere. Then, as I was crossing the street, I happened to see a cab sitting at a red light a couple
blocks down. And I thought — now *that* is a story . . . a perfect little story capsule on wheels, rolling along Third Avenue. Inside, there's
a character, and that character wants something, wants to get somewhere. That could be my novel, right there . . . only how will I ever
meet that person, learn that story? And then, suddenly, it hit me!
The cab, that is. This girl came running over — "Omigosh, omigosh,
I'm so sorry!" Apparently she was in the cab and she saw some friends
of hers on the corner of 72nd and 3rd. She got excited and yelled
out something that distracted the driver. It was the first time she'd
ever taken a cab and she swore she'd never do it again because this
was all her fault. I kept telling her I wasn't hurt, in fact, I said I ought
to thank her — because as I was lying there, it came to me . . . not

just the opening line, but the whole first scene! I think it was there all along; it just needed to be knocked loose. Anyway, she seemed really nice. And we're having lunch next week so I can show her a draft of chapter one. Strange, but hey — you never know how these things are gonna happen.

TEXAS HOMOS
Jan Buttram

Seriocomic
Cecil, forties

> *This comedy takes place in a moderately sized city in Texas. Cecil*
> *is a doctor, and one of the wealthiest men in town. He's in quite a*
> *predicament, because he's been arrested for solicitation in the men's*
> *room of a local park. He could lose his wife and his lucrative med-*
> *ical practice. He is scheming about how to beat the rap. He has had*
> *an idea about how to blackmail the judge who will hear his case.*
> *He starts out talking to Harold D., his lawyer, who is not sure Cecil*
> *can escape his predicament. He then gets on the phone to his*
> *secretary.*

CECIL: *(To Harold D.)* I'll take you down with me, boy. Just remember,
I hold a lien on this goddamn office . . . I'll jog Judge Peters' mem-
ory bank. You settle this before the damn Longhorns kickoff! . . .
(Cecil dials the phone.) Loretta. I need you to get over to the office, pronto! Pull up the file on Candy Jones. I saw her a couple of
years back . . . Xerox it and fax it over to Judge Gerald Peters . . . I
know it's confidential information, that's the point . . . no
message . . . just the medical record, and get me last year's total con-
tributions I made to the Democrats and the Republicans . . .
(A beat.)
What? When did that come in? God almighty! No, I didn't get
the message. Because I don't have my goddamn cell phone . . . I know
my language has gone all to hell . . . E-mail her chart over to Dr.
Brewer. Reschedule all my appointments. Loretta, stop questioning
me or find a new job, and good luck on finding one that pays as
much as you're making now.
(Cecil disconnects the phone. Dials a number.)
Bobby? How's it going, pal? Listen, I need you to cover my

rounds today. I was arrested. I was driving home last night and I had to take a dump, so I stopped in the park because I was about to poop my pants, and I walked into this homosexual ring and the police had some sting happening, and those idiots handcuffed me and threw me in the lockup. Hell, yes, I told them who I am. I didn't do a damn thing except look at this Mexican kid kinda funny when he asked me if he could suck my dick. You know I always have to protect my hands so I couldn't just sock the shit out of him, and I guess he took that as a "yes." Harold D. is getting the charges dismissed. Now, Mrs. Adele Potts has got a tumor the size of a golf ball in her abdomen that's causing some bowel blockage. It's benign but painful as hell. I had scheduled some surgery Monday afternoon . . . sounds like it may be more pressing. Yeah, the shit is backing up. Well, just see her and don't let her take any of that homeopathic crap. Sweet talk her. I know you don't like to do that but she's my girl, so sugar coat it. Yeah, thanks. Loretta will e-mail you the other patients. Well, just read the paper . . . and, do you believe, Jim Bob is here with me and he's innocent, too.

(Gives thumbs up to Jim Bob.)

And they got that poor little Delbert Simmons kid. Hell, yes, he's innocent.

(Gives thumbs up to Delbert.)

We just walked in and they slapped cuffs on us. That Supreme Court has turned them hysterical. Hell, I don't blame 'em either, if you can't get rid of the queers one way, get 'em another way. But these yokels took civilian casualties. It's going to be one hellava lawsuit before I'm finished.

So, if you talk to anyone, we were framed. Out and out framed. You got it. I'll be there for you next time . . .

TEXAS HOMOS
Jan Buttram

Dramatic
Jim Bob, forties

> *Jim Bob, a preacher and married with a family, has been arrested
> for solicitation in the men's room of a park in a small Texas city. He
> is talking to Cecil — a doctor, who has also been arrested, and who
> wants them to band together to beat the rap — about the epiphany
> he has experienced as a result of his arrest.*

JIM BOB: I walked out of that bathroom last night in handcuffs, and I was
giddy. My legs were trembling. The policeman placed his hand on
my head, guiding me into the back seat of the police car, and it was
like he was blessing me . . . I felt the steel handcuffs dig into my
wrists. I thought, I have finally done it . . . I forced God's hand to
reach down from heaven and say, "This is it, Jim Bob . . . you're
mine." . . .

I've had a wonderful life so far, and I'm grateful for it . . . but
it's all been preparation for this moment. Because the truth is, I've
always been afraid of people knowing the real me. Cecil, God's truth,
you're the only person who knows who I am. And last night, praying with Wally . . .

(Looking at the newspaper.)

Where is he . . . there's his name, Wally Byrd . . . solicitation
and indecent exposure . . . his name was Wally Byrd . . . when I was
helping Wally find the Lord . . . it was like I was talking to you, Cecil.
Even though I'd just met him, Wally knew me, he knew me like the
Lord has always known me . . . because Wally and I were in the same
jail for the same reason. And we prayed long and hard, and in the
prayer, I was walking along a road in Jerusalem and I met Jesus, face-
to-face. And Jesus held up his hand and stopped me. He spoke to
me, and when he spoke to me, I spoke to Wally Byrd. I said, "Wally
Byrd, here's your chance to leave uncertainty behind. There's a greater

picture, a larger version of you and me and the Lord wants the world to know the truth of who we are." . . .

Cecil, last night I found myself. I found me, the man I would like to be. I was out in the open for everyone to see. I felt a relief, a weight lifted from me . . .

TEXAS HOMOS
Jan Buttram

Dramatic
Cecil, forties

> *Cecil, a very successful doctor in a small Texas city, married with*
> *children, has been arrested for solicitation in the men's room of a*
> *local park, along with Jim Bob, a long-time friend, who's a minis-*
> *ter, also married with children. Cecil has been scheming the whole*
> *play as to how to beat the rap. Here, Jim Bob has confessed his love*
> *for him, which he cannot reciprocate, because to do so would mean*
> *admitting the truth about himself — which would mean the loss*
> *of his wife and his lucrative medical practice.*

CECIL: Are you laughing or crying?

(No answer.)

Good God, Jim Bob. I wish I could help you out, buddy. I wish
I could snap my fingers and feel a different way. You just never talked
to me about any of this. You just presumed that I was taking this se-
riously. I never did. I'm sorry. I'm just overwhelmed with this serious turn you've taken here and . . . damn, I'm grateful that somebody
loves me, I am. I mean, thank you . . .

(A beat.)

Jim Bob, you're just worried about Tulie and all this shit. Look,
I'm going to find us a way out. We'll wind up this thing pretty quick.
Grab a shower, get some clean clothes. Find our cars. I'll get Tulie
transferred to a private room on my ward. She'll be all right. We can
order in a couple of pizzas, watch the game at the hospital . . .

You're just in a mood. Moody since the first damn grade. A
preacher can't afford to be moody. It's lucky you're a part-time ac-
countant. I'm prescribing a complete physical for you once we get
through this.

(No response.)

Look. You want me to say I was scared? I was scared. Last night I was scared. Those other men in the cell scared the shit out of me. I mean, I like sex but I like it on my terms, not somebody else's. So, I was scared.

(A moment.)

Just settle down, now. You don't want Delbert to see you like this. And Harold D., Christ, if Judy Kay comes in, she'll have a field day.

TO MOSCOW!
Jeanmarie Williams

Dramatic

History Teacher, could be any age or any sex

A history teacher is addressing his (or her) class.

HISTORY TEACHER: And so we find, of course, that Time is a line. Time, as we know, as we've all *suspected* for millions of years, is a line with two points that stretch out on into Infinity — now there's a word — Infinity, until Time will stop, which of course, we know it will not.

The religious among you may ask, yes, but what about God? What about that glorious first moment and the inevitable last? I offer for your consideration the idea that, truth be told, yes, that this book you read with such fervor and passion, is not a map, no, a violent *tool,* perhaps, but definitely, merely, at last, a guide. And that's all I have to say about that.

Now some of you are thinking right now, wandering off as it were, seeing visions of circles and continuumzzz of your own, constructing little epi-sssodes and intrigues, perhaps about some alternative geometric theory, some loop that folds back onto itself. And maverick though you be, I tell you this. You are also wrong.

Think about yesterday and then consider today. Imagine tomorrow. Buck up. You are not lost. You can find yourself if you place yourself on the line. Get in line, little soldiers, get in line. Get in line and look to the right. Look ahead. See yourself on the line. Where are you going? Where will you end up? On the line. Where have you been? What have you done? Look to the left. See yourself there as you were. You've been on the line this whole time.

I know this is comforting to you. It's comforting to me as well. Can we ask any more from History? Can we ask for any more comfort than this?

TUMOR
Sheila Callaghan

Dramatic
Richard, twenty-five to thirty

Richard has been fighting with his wife over the TV remote. This is direct address to the audience.

RICHARD: I'm lying on the basement floor of my parent's house at 4 A.M. and I'm completely fucked up, all kinds of unbelievable shit jacking through me, and the phone rings, it's Kathie, she's completely fucked up too, and bored, and she goes "Wanna get married." So I'm like OK, next thing I know we're in a cab on our way to the airport for a 6:30 flight to Vegas. And we're in the back of the cab tearing and clawing at each other, screaming laughing, I've got her panties hanging from my ear . . . It was fucking epic.

But we get to the airport and we're at the terminal waiting for our flight, she's got this screeching grin stuck to her face like a postage stamp, I'm squinting from the glare and I start to feel this sour thing happen in my throat.

But we do it anyway. It isn't bad, at first. We still get fucked up, we still have fun. She's a lot more laid-back than my first two wives. The she starts in with "We need a dog, we NEED a dog, we gotta get one NOW" and her eyes are all twinkly and maternal, what the fuck do I care, a dog, great, love dogs, bring it on. No idea what I'm in for. Walking cleaning washing feeding fetching training picking up doody with paper towels in every fucking room because the damn animal thinks it's funny to watch me clean up its doody, and frankly I don't blame him but it's still a downright mean existence.

Then she tells me she's pregnant. I'm shocked, I mean I never used a thingie because you know we were married and I thought she had that all taken care of. She suddenly becomes this angry angry woman, she's angry at me every single day, it's incredible, and the dog becomes the centerpiece of our misery. I'm not taking care of him right, I'm not playing with him enough, I'm leaving the doody in the living room for too many days, and I'm thinking, what the fuck is gonna happen with a BABY?

TWENTIETH CENTURY
Adapted by Ken Ludwig from the play by
Ben Hecht and Charles MacArthur

Comic
Oscar Jaffe, forties

> *Jaffe is a practically insolvent Broadway producer. He hopes to re-*
> *vive his fortunes by persuading Broadway star Lily Garland to ap-*
> *pear in his next production — improbably, a dramatization of the*
> *story of Christ, with Lily as Mary Magdalene. Lily, who has been*
> *burned more than once by Oscar, both professionally and romanti-*
> *cally, is, shall we say, extremely dubious. Here, Oscar tries to sell her*
> *on the production.*

JAFFE: Lily, that's it! You have it! I see the whole thing. I see the Magdalene as a fine, aristocratic woman with folds of silk framing her forehead. Then, after being heartbroken by someone she loves, she goes
down, down into the depths . . . I'm going to make it my greatest
production ever. I've brought over an entire troupe from Europe —
I flew to Nuremberg to find them. Lily, I've run the figures. If the
play runs for five years I won't make a cent. You can have all the
money. I only want to stagger New York. I want a desert scene with
real camels and sand from the Holy Land. *(He starts pacing.)* I'll have
a banquet that you give for your lover in the Second Act. Pontius
Pilate, Governor of Judea. You have your slaves all around you, and
you're covered in emeralds from head to foot without a stitch of cloth-
ing underneath. "Pontius, why do you stare at me. Have you not seen
my gems before?" Your skin is like porcelain, almost transparent in
its fineness — think of Michelangelo, the Piéta. Pilate begs you to
marry him and you laugh in his face, haha!, despising men for what
they did to you. Your cruel, terrible laughter rings through the palace
and makes his blood run cold. "My blood, it's cold." But that's nothing compared to the finish, where you stand in rags in the anteroom

and the Emperor Nero himself offers you half his empire. You answer him with a speech that may be the greatest piece of literature ever written, with the sun pouring down on you, transfigured with love and sacrifice! "Never!" you cry. "Never will I betray the love and trust of he who loves and trusts us all!" Nero cringes! — you push him away! — "Ha!" — and the last we see of you, as the curtain falls, is this pathetic little figure in the distance, selling olives in the market place. "Olives . . . olives . . . Three for a drachma . . . Olives . . ." *(He bows his head in conclusion.)*

THE VIOLET HOUR
Richard Greenberg

Dramatic
Denny, late twenties

> *Denny is an F. Scott Fitzgerald sort, an aspiring novelist desperate for success — as a novelist and in romance. He is desperately in love with Rosamund, a wealthy girl whose father will not allow him to marry her unless he can demonstrate financial success. He is talking to John, an old college chum who has started up a new publishing house.*

DENNY: I saw that it had rained again, lightly, and the rain had cooled the air and puddled the street with these tiny, skittish oil paintings, and I wasn't hungry anymore, and my body didn't ache, and I thought yes —

and I thought *no* —
and I thought *yes* –
Rosamund had happened.

Then clerks and secretaries started to emerge from office buildings and scurry every which way and the daylight dimmed and the neon lights switched on and people's reflections dappled in store windows and I thought: This is the violet hour!

And I thought: *That's* my title!

And for the first time that day, I was altogether present. I had no money — I would have to walk home over the Queensborough Bridge, but I didn't despair as I usually did because I knew — I *knew* — I would only be crossing this bridge a few more times, and suddenly I was inside my horrible little apartment. I stripped naked and got into bed and melted to sleep and slept seventeen hours and the next day I arrived at work four hours late and showered my boss with obscenities. *(Pause.)* So you see, you *have* to publish me, or my happiness is ended.

WHAT THE NIGHT IS FOR
Michael Weller

Dramatic
Adam, forties

Adam has run into Lindy, an old love. They are in a hotel room, considering reviving their romance, which ended long ago.

ADAM: We vowed we'd always have each other while the rest of our life went on. It was a marriage, Lindy. A secret marriage. . . .

I've thought a lot about that idea over the years. More and more in fact. What a good thing it might have been — . . .

No, I've *seen* it. My partner's dad comes to town on business a couple three times a year and once up in Riverdale way off the beaten path, inspecting a job site, I saw him go into a restaurant with his arm around this plump smiley white-haired lady with pink cheeks, you know, wire rim glasses, one of those jolly-sexy older liberal lady types. Herman turned and saw me. He's married, you see. I know his wife. She's great. They're a total family-family. My partner still thinks growing up with them ruined his chances for marriage because he'll never be as happy with someone as his folks are with each other, and it's true, they're happy. But there's his old dad — oh, right; six months later he treated our office to dinner, he's in town with *his wife* this time, and when I go in the men's room he's right behind me, boom, to the next stall. "The woman you saw me with, we've been lovers for thirty-seven years. No one knows, not even my kid, you got that?" and he walks out. I found him back at the table with his arm around his wife . . . he loves her, too. Herman is an ordinary guy. Husband, provider — solid citizen. It's *not* a fairy tale. . . .

I want you back.

111

York, NY 10010. The entire text has been published in an acting edition by Dramatists Play Service, which also handles performance rights. Contact: Dramatists Play Service, 440 Park Ave. S., New York, NY 10016, www.dramatists.com, 212-MU3-8960.

A NERVOUS SMILE. ©2005 by John Belluso. Reprinted by permission of International Creative Management, 40 W. 57th St., New York, NY 10019. The entire text has been published by Smith and Kraus in *Humana Festival 2005: The Complete Plays,* and in an acting edition by Dramatists Play Service, Inc., 440 Park Avenue South, New York, NY 10016. www.dramatists.com, 212-MU3-8960. Contact Dramatists Play Service for performance rights.

THE PEOPLE VS. SPAM. ©2004 by Jonathan Rand. Reprinted by permission of Playscripts, Inc., which has published the entire text in an acting edition and which handles performance rights. Contact: Playscripts, Inc., Box 237060, New York, NY 10023, www.playscripts.com, 866-NEW-PLAY.

PLATONOV! PLATONOV! PLATONOV! ©2005 by Eric Michael Kochmer. Reprinted by permission of the author. The entire text has been published by New York Theatre Experience (www.newyorktheatreexperience.org) in *Plays and Playwrights 2005.*

PORTRAITS. ©2002 by Jonathan Bell. Reprinted by permission of Ronald Feiner, Kaufman, Feiner, Yamin, Gilden & Robbins, 777 3rd Ave., New York, NY 10017. The entire text has been published in an acting edition by Samuel French, Inc., which also handles performance rights. Contact: Samuel French, Inc., 45 W. 25th St., New York, NY 10010, www.samuelfrench.com, 212-206-8990.

PURE CONFIDENCE. ©2003 by Carlyle Brown. Reprinted by permission of Bret Adams Ltd., 448 W. 44th St., New York, NY 10036. Contact Bret Adams Ltd. for performance rights. The entire text has been published by Smith and Kraus in *Humana Festival 2005: The Complete Plays.*

SMALL TRAGEDY. ©2005 by Craig Lucas. Reprinted by permission of William Morris Agency, Inc., 1325 Ave. of the Americas, New York, NY 10019. The entire text has been published in an acting edition by Samuel French, Inc., which also handles performance rights. Contact: Samuel French, Inc., 45 W. 25th St., New York, NY 10010, www.samuelfrench.com, 212-206-8990.

THE TAXI CABARET. ©2000, 2004 by Peter Mills. Reprinted by permission of the Susan Gurman Agency, L.L.C. 865 West End Ave. #15A, New York,